DBT

Christian Companion

Linda Houts, MSW, LCSW

DBT

Christian Companion

This publication is designed to provide accurate and authoritative information concerning the subject matter covered for educational purposes. It is sold with the understanding that the publisher is not engaged in rendering psychological, financial, legal, or other professional service. If you have questions or concerns about your emotional or medical well-being, seek expert assistance of a competent mental health or medical professional.

The views expressed in this work are solely those of the author. Reproduction for client use is authorized. Any other reproduction in any form is prohibited without the express written permission of the author.

Distributed by Amazon Kindle Direct Publishing

ISBN: 9798878541503

Contents

Special Note from the Author

I began my DBT journey at Heartland Behavioral Health Services in Nevada, Missouri. During my time at Heartland, I participated with the DBT team in obtaining 65 postgraduate DBT intensive training hours from Behavior Tech while providing care to children, adolescents, and their families. I developed, and implemented a residential DBT program for adolescent males before moving to community mental health. I practiced for a short time in a multidisciplinary family practice clinic before filling a much-needed position in Senior Life Solutions (SLS) Intensive Outpatient (IOP) geriatric psychiatric program treating older adults, before beginning my current practice in a multidisciplinary family practice providing psychotherapy to patients of all ages.

This volume is intended as a desk reference for providers, and a daily resource for patients using DBT. I suggest highlighting the verses that speak most to you, when there are multiple verse offerings for a skill. I am not a clergy or specialist in Bible studies.

Many thanks to those who have supported me in my journey and this endeavor including patients and their families for allowing me to sit with you and walk with you through your recovery. My father and daughter for their never ending loving support. Many thanks also go to Dr. Conrad Gubera, whose ability to provide context to the disparate set a foundation for my critical thinking about social contexts and conditions that affect the human condition. Dr. Renee White, without whom I would not be a Social Worker, one of the great passions of my life! Susie Platt, LCSW and Alyson Harder, LCSW, LSCSW, Chief Executive Officer Heartland Behavioral Health Services for their devotion to the next generations of social workers including myself.

I would love to hear your thoughts, feedback and any questions you may have. I invite you leave a review at your place of purchase. Connect with me at www.linkedin.com/in/Linda-Houts-Lcsw , www.facebook.com/LindaHoutsMswLcsw or www.facebook.com/groups/PracticalDBT .

Chapter 1

Mindfulness

How Skills

To live fully, DBT encourages us to be non-judgmental, mindful of the moment, and to focus on the desired outcome for each situation (Linehan, 2014).

How A³

A   Awareness   Proverbs 14:8 ESV The wisdom of the prudent is to discern his
                     way, but the folly of fools is deceiving.

                     Psalm 26:2 ESV Prove me, O LORD, and try me; test my heart and
                     my mind.

                     1 John 1:8 ESV If we say we have no sin, we deceive ourselves,
                     and the truth is not in us.

                     Romans 8:7 ESV For the mind that is set on the flesh is hostile to
                     God, for it does not submit to God's law; indeed, it cannot.

A   Acceptance   Romans 12:2 ESV Do not be conformed to this world, but be
                     transformed by the renewal of your mind, that by testing you may
                     discern what is the will of God, what is good and acceptable and
                     perfect.

                     Isaiah 41:10 ESV Fear not, for I am with you; be not dismayed, for
                     I am your God; I will strengthen you, I will help you, I will uphold
                     you with my righteous right hand.

                     Matthew 11:28 ESV Come to me, all who labor and are heavy
                     laden, and I will give you rest.

A   Action   James 2:24 ESV You see that a person is justified by works and
                     not by faith alone.

1 Thessalonians 5:21 ESV But test everything; hold fast what is good.

Proverbs 20:11 ESV

Even a child makes himself known by his acts, by whether his conduct is pure and upright.

2 Timothy 1:7 ESV

For God gave us a spirit not of fear but of power and love and self-control.

Romans 8:28 ESV

And we know that for those who love God all things work together for good, for those who are called according to his purpose.

Non-Judgment

Taking a non-judgmental stance means – do not judge things as good or bad, right or wrong.	Luke 6:37 ESV Judge not, and you will not be judged; condemn not, and you will not be condemned; forgive, and you will be forgiven;
It is effective to focus on the consequence of behavior instead of judging others or ourselves.	Psalm 119:1-176 ESV Blessed are those whose way is blameless, who walk in the law of the Lord! Blessed are those who keep his testimonies, who seek him with their whole heart, who also do no wrong, but walk in his ways! You have commanded your precepts to be kept diligently. Oh that my ways may be steadfast in keeping your statutes! ...
It is helpful to fully describe what is observed and collect just the facts; without judging those involved or the circumstances.	John 17:17 ESV Sanctify them in the truth; your word is truth.

One Mindful

non-judgmentally   Luke 6:37 ESV "Judge not, and you will not be judged; condemn not, and you will not be condemned; forgive, and you will be forgiven;

one-mindfully   Philippians 2:2 ESV Complete my joy by being of the same mind, having the same love, being in full accord and of one mind.

effectively   Colossians 3:17 ESV And whatever you do, in word or deed, do everything in the name of the Lord Jesus, giving thanks to God the Father through him.

         James 1:5 ESV If any of you lacks wisdom, let him ask God, who gives generously to all without reproach, and it will be given him.

         James 3:17 ESV

         But the wisdom from above is first pure, then peaceable, gentle, open to reason, full of mercy and good fruits, impartial and sincere.

What Skills

DBT encourages us to live our lives fully. To do so, it's most effective
to: observe, describe, and participate in the activity of the moment throughout our day
(Linehan, 2014).

Observe

Pay attention to events, emotions, and thoughts.   1 Timothy 4:15-16, NIV: "Be diligent in these matters and absorbed in them, so that your progress will be evident to all. Pay close attention to your life and to your teaching. Persevere in these things, for by so doing you will save both yourself and those who hear you."

Hebrews 2:1, ESV: "Therefore we must pay much closer attention to what we have heard, lest we drift away from it."

Try not to terminate them when they are painful.

Psalms 147:3 - He healeth the broken in heart, and bindeth up their wounds.

John 14:27 - Peace I leave with you, my peace I give unto you: not as the world giveth, give I unto you. Let not your heart be troubled, neither let it be afraid.

Try not to prolong them when they are pleasant.

James 1:19-20 ESV Know this, my beloved brothers: let every person be quick to hear, slow to speak, slow to anger; for the anger of man does not produce the righteousness of God.

Colossians 3:8 ESV But now you must put them all away: anger, wrath, malice, slander, and obscene talk from your mouth.

Proverbs 16:32 ESV Whoever is slow to anger is better than the mighty, and he who rules his spirit than he who takes a city.

Proverbs 15:1 ESV A soft answer turns away wrath, but a harsh word stirs up anger.

3 John 1:2 ESV Beloved, I pray that all may go well with you and that you may be in good health, as it goes well with your soul.

1 John 1:9 ESV If we confess our sins, he is faithful and just to forgive us our sins and to cleanse us from all unrighteousness.

2 Timothy 3:16 ESV All Scripture is breathed out by God and profitable for teaching, for reproof, for correction, and for training in righteousness,

Allow yourself to experience with awareness.

Philippians 4:6-7 ESV Do not be anxious about anything, but in everything by prayer and supplication with thanksgiving let your requests be made known to God. And the peace of God, which surpasses all understanding, will guard your hearts and your minds in Christ Jesus.

Romans 8:28 ESV And we know that for those who love God all things work together for good, for those who are called according to his purpose.

Galatians 5:22-23 ESV But the fruit of the Spirit is love, joy, peace, patience, kindness, goodness, faithfulness, gentleness, self-control; against such things there is no law.

Psalm 147:3 ESV He heals the brokenhearted and binds up their wounds.

Describe

Describe events, label emotions, and identify thoughts.

Proverbs 4:23 ESV Keep your heart with all vigilance, for from it flow the springs of life.

| Try not to take emotions and thoughts as accurate and exact reflections of events. | 2 Timothy 2:15 NIV Do your best to present yourself to God as one approved, a worker who does not need to be ashamed and who correctly handles the word of truth. |
| List "just the facts" – No need to label or judge. | Luke 6:37 ESV Judge not, and you will not be judged; condemn not, and you will not be condemned; forgive, and you will be forgiven; |

Participate

Enter completely into the activity of the moment.	Philippians 4:6-7 NIV Do not be anxious about anything, but in every situation, by prayer and petition, with thanksgiving, present your requests to God. And the peace of God, which transcends all understanding, will guard your hearts and your minds in Christ Jesus.
Try not to be self-conscious.	Romans 12:3 ESV For by the grace given to me I say to everyone among you not to think of himself more highly than he ought to think, but to think with sober judgment, each according to the measure of faith that God has assigned.
	2 Corinthians 13:5 ESV Examine yourselves, to see whether you are in the faith. Test yourselves. Or do you not realize this about yourselves, that Jesus Christ is in you?—unless indeed you fail to meet the test!
Be spontaneous and give attention to the activity.	Ecclesiastes 3:13 ESV Also that everyone should eat and drink and take pleasure in all his toil—this is God's gift to man.
	Ecclesiastes 2:24 ESV There is nothing better for a person than that he should eat and drink and find

enjoyment in his toil. This also, I saw, is from the hand of God,

Colossians 3:17 ESV And whatever you do, in word or deed, do everything in the name of the Lord Jesus, giving thanks to God the Father through him.

2 Timothy 2:15 ESV Do your best to present yourself to God as one approved, a worker who has no need to be ashamed, rightly handling the word of truth.

Discernment

Discernment is the term is the spiritual characteristic of making thoughtful thinking about the truth. In other words Wise Mind.

1 Corinthians 11:1 ESV Be imitators of me, as I am of Christ.

1 Corinthians 12:10 ESV To another the working of miracles, to another prophecy, to another the ability to distinguish between spirits, to another various kinds of tongues, to another the interpretation of tongues.

1 Corinthians 12:11 ESV All these are empowered by one and the same Spirit, who apportions to each one individually as he wills.

1 Corinthians 13:12 ESV For now we see in a mirror dimly, but then face to face. Now I know in part; then I shall know fully, even as I have been fully known.

1 Corinthians 14:33 ESV For God is not a God of confusion but of peace. As in all the churches of the saints,

1 Corinthians 2:11 ESV For who knows a person's thoughts except the spirit of that person, which is in him? So also no one comprehends the thoughts of God except the Spirit of God.

1 Corinthians 2:1-16 ESV And I, when I came to you, brothers, did not come proclaiming to you the testimony of God with lofty speech or wisdom. For I decided to know nothing among you except Jesus Christ and him crucified. And I was with you in weakness and in fear and much trembling, and my speech and my message were not in plausible words of wisdom, but in demonstration of the Spirit and of power, so that your faith might not rest in the wisdom of men but in the power of God. ...

1 Corinthians 2:14 ESV The natural person does not accept the things of the Spirit of God, for they are folly to him, and he is not able to understand them because they are spiritually discerned.

1 Corinthians 2:16 ESV "For who has understood the mind of the Lord so as to instruct him?" But we have the mind of Christ.

1 John 2:27 ESV But the anointing that you received from him abides in you, and you have no need that anyone should teach you. But as his anointing teaches you about everything, and is true, and is no lie—just as it has taught you, abide in him.

1 John 3:2 ESV Beloved, we are God's children now, and what we will be has not yet appeared; but we know that when he appears we shall be like him, because we shall see him as he is.

1 John 3:4 ESV Everyone who makes a practice of sinning also practices lawlessness; sin is lawlessness.

1 John 4:1 ESV Beloved, do not believe every spirit, but test the spirits to see whether they are from God, for many false prophets have gone out into the world.

1 Kings 3:11 ESV 1 Kings 3:9 ESV Give your servant therefore an understanding mind to govern your people, that I may discern between good and evil, for who is able to govern this your great people?"

1 Thessalonians 5:21 ESV But test everything; hold fast what is good.

1 Timothy 6:3-5 ESV If anyone teaches a different doctrine and does not agree with the sound words of our Lord Jesus Christ and the teaching that accords with godliness, he is puffed up with conceit and understands nothing. He has an unhealthy craving for controversy and for quarrels about words, which produce envy, dissension, slander, evil suspicions, and constant friction among people who are depraved in mind and deprived of the truth, imagining that godliness is a means of gain.

2 Corinthians 10:3-5 ESV For though we walk in the flesh, we are not waging war according to the flesh. For the weapons of our warfare are not of the flesh but have divine power to destroy strongholds. We destroy arguments and every lofty opinion raised against the knowledge of God, and take every thought captive to obey Christ,

2 Corinthians 7:1 ESV Since we have these promises, beloved, let us cleanse ourselves from every defilement of body and spirit, bringing holiness to completion in the fear of God.

Colossians 2:8 ESV See to it that no one takes you captive by philosophy and empty deceit, according to human tradition, according to the elemental spirits of the world, and not according to Christ.

Daniel 2:21 ESV He changes times and seasons; he removes kings and sets up kings; he gives wisdom to the wise and knowledge to those who have understanding;

Deuteronomy 32:28-29 ESV For they are a nation void of counsel, and there is no understanding in them. If they were wise, they would understand this; they would discern their latter end!

Ezekiel 44:23 ESV They shall teach my people the difference between the holy and the common, and show them how to distinguish between the unclean and the clean.

Hebrews 4:12 ESV For the word of God is living and active, sharper than any two-edged sword, piercing to the division of soul and of spirit, of joints and of marrow, and discerning the thoughts and intentions of the heart.

Hebrews 5:14 ESV But solid food is for the mature, for those who have their powers of discernment trained by constant practice to distinguish good from evil.

Hosea 14:9 ESV Whoever is wise, let him understand these things; whoever is discerning, let him know them; for the ways of the LORD are right, and the upright walk in them, but transgressors stumble in them.

Isaiah 11:3 ESV And his delight shall be in the fear of the LORD. He shall not judge by what his eyes see, or decide disputes by what his ears hear,

Isaiah 59:2 ESV But your iniquities have made a separation between you and your God, and your sins have hidden his face from you so that he does not hear.

Isaiah 7:15 ESV He shall eat curds and honey when he knows how to refuse the evil and choose the good.

James 1:5 ESV If any of you lacks wisdom, let him ask God, who gives generously to all without reproach, and it will be given him.

James 3:17 ESV But the wisdom from above is first pure, then peaceable, gentle, open to reason, full of mercy and good fruits, impartial and sincere.

Jeremiah 23:5 ESV Behold, the days are coming, declares the LORD, when I will raise up for David a righteous Branch, and he shall reign as king and deal wisely, and shall execute justice and righteousness in the land.

John 15:26 ESV "But when the Helper comes, whom I will send to you from the Father, the Spirit of truth, who proceeds from the Father, he will bear witness about me.

John 16:13 ESV When the Spirit of truth comes, he will guide you into all the truth, for he will not speak on his own authority, but whatever he hears he will speak, and he will declare to you the things that are to come.

John 17:17 ESV Sanctify them in the truth; your word is truth.

John 21:17 ESV He said to him the third time, "Simon, son of John, do you love me?" Peter was grieved because he said to him the third time, "Do you love me?" and he said to him, "Lord, you know everything; you know that I love you." Jesus said to him, "Feed my sheep.

John 7:24 ESV Do not judge by appearances, but judge with right judgment."

Matthew 16:3 ESV And in the morning, 'It will be stormy today, for the sky is red and threatening.' You know how to interpret the appearance of the sky, but you cannot interpret the signs of the times.

Matthew 24:32-33 ESV "From the fig tree learn its lesson: as soon as its branch becomes tender and puts out its leaves, you know that summer is near. So also, when you see all these things, you know that he is near, at the very gates.

Matthew 24:45 ESV "Who then is the faithful and wise servant, whom his master has set over his household, to give them their food at the proper time?

Matthew 24:4-5 ESV And Jesus answered them, "See that no one leads you astray. For many will come in my name, saying, 'I am the Christ,' and they will lead many astray.

Matthew 5:8 ESV "Blessed are the pure in heart, for they shall see God.

Matthew 6:22 ESV "The eye is the lamp of the body. So, if your eye is healthy, your whole body will be full of light,

Philippians 1:9 ESV And it is my prayer that your love may abound more and more, with knowledge and all discernment,

Philippians 1:9-10 ESV And it is my prayer that your love may abound more and more, with knowledge and all discernment, so that you may approve what is excellent, and so be pure and blameless for the day of Christ,

Philippians 1:9-11 ESV And it is my prayer that your love may abound more and more, with knowledge and all discernment, so that you may approve what is excellent, and so be pure and blameless for the day of Christ, filled with the fruit of righteousness that comes through Jesus Christ, to the glory and praise of God.

Proverbs 1:5 ESV Let the wise hear and increase in learning, and the one who understands obtain guidance,

Proverbs 14:6 ESV A scoffer seeks wisdom in vain, but knowledge is easy for a man of understanding.

Proverbs 15:14 ESV The heart of him who has understanding seeks knowledge, but the mouths of fools feed on folly.

Proverbs 15:21 ESV Folly is a joy to him who lacks sense, but a man of understanding walks straight ahead.

Proverbs 17:24 ESV The discerning sets his face toward wisdom, but the eyes of a fool are on the ends of the earth.

Proverbs 18:15 ESV An intelligent heart acquires knowledge, and the ear of the wise seeks knowledge.

Proverbs 19:25 ESV Strike a scoffer, and the simple will learn prudence; reprove a man of understanding, and he will gain knowledge.

Proverbs 2:1-5 ESV My son, if you receive my words and treasure up my commandments with you, making your ear attentive to wisdom and inclining your heart to understanding; yes, if you call out for insight and raise your voice for understanding, if you seek it like silver and search for it as for hidden treasures, then you will understand the fear of the LORD and find the knowledge of God.

Proverbs 2:3-5 ESV Yes, if you call out for insight and raise your voice for understanding, if you seek it like silver and search for it as for hidden treasures, then you will understand the fear of the LORD and find the knowledge of God.

Proverbs 3:13 ESV Blessed is the one who finds wisdom, and the one who gets understanding,

Proverbs 3:21 ESV My son, do not lose sight of these— keep sound wisdom and discretion,

Proverbs 4:7 ESV The beginning of wisdom is this: Get wisdom, and whatever you get, get insight.

Psalm 119:125 ESV I am your servant; give me understanding, that I may know your testimonies!

Psalm 119:66 ESV Teach me good judgment and knowledge, for I believe in your commandments.

Psalm 23:1-6 ESV A Psalm of David. The LORD is my shepherd; I shall not want. He makes me lie down in green pastures. He leads me beside still waters. He restores my soul. He leads me in paths of righteousness for his name's sake. Even though I walk through the valley of the shadow of death, I will fear no evil, for you are with me; your rod and your staff, they comfort me. You prepare a table before me in the presence of my enemies; you anoint my head with oil; my cup overflows. ...

Romans 12:2 ESV Do not be conformed to this world, but be transformed by the renewal of your mind, that by testing you may discern what is the will of God, what is good and acceptable and perfect.

DBT encourages us to be mindful of our thoughts to manage them effectively (Linehan, 2014).

Turn the Mind

Romans 12:2 ESV Do not be conformed to this world, but be transformed by the renewal of your mind, that by testing you may discern what is the will of God, what is good and acceptable and perfect.

Philippians 4:8 ESV Finally, brothers, whatever is true, whatever is honorable, whatever is just, whatever is pure, whatever is lovely, whatever is commendable, if there is any excellence, if there is anything worthy of praise, think about these things.

Colossians 3:2 ESV Set your minds on things that are above, not on things that are on earth.

Ephesians 4:23 ESV And to be renewed in the spirit of your minds,

Matthew 26:41 ESV Watch and pray that you may not enter into temptation. The spirit indeed is willing, but the flesh is weak.

Philippians 2:13 ESV For it is God who works in you, both to will and to work for his good pleasure.

2 Corinthians 8:11 ESV So now finish doing it as well, so that your readiness in desiring it may be matched by your completing it out of what you have.

Isaiah 1:20 ESV But if you refuse and rebel, you shall be eaten by the sword; for the mouth of the LORD has spoken."

Radical
Acceptance

Philippians 4:8 ESV Finally, brothers, whatever is true, whatever is honorable, whatever is just, whatever is pure, whatever is lovely, whatever is commendable, if there is any excellence, if there is anything worthy of praise, think about these things.

Job 38:36 ESV Who has put wisdom in the inward parts or given understanding to the mind?

Hebrews 11:1 ESV Now faith is the assurance of things hoped for, the conviction of things not seen.

1 Thessalonians 5:21 ESV But test everything; hold fast what is good.

Romans 8:28 ESV And we know that for those who love God all things work together for good, for those who are called according to his purpose.

Ephesians 2:10 ESV/For we are his workmanship, created in Christ Jesus for good works, which God prepared beforehand, that we should walk in them.

Ecclesiastes 3:1 ESV For everything there is a season, and a time for every matter under heaven:

1 Corinthians 13:4-5 ESV Love is patient and kind; love does not envy or boast; it is not arrogant or rude. It does not insist on its own way; it is not irritable or resentful;

Psalm 121:2 ESV My help comes from the LORD, who made heaven and earth.

Jeremiah 29:11 ESV For I know the plans I have for you, declares the LORD, plans for welfare and not for evil, to give you a future and a hope.

Willingness

2 Corinthians 8:12 ESV For if the readiness is there, it is acceptable according to what a person has, not according to what he does not have.

Ephesians 6:7 ESV Rendering service with a good will as to the Lord and not to man,

Isaiah 1:19 ESV If you are willing and obedient, you shall eat the good of the land;

Matthew 26:41 ESV Watch and pray that you may not enter into temptation. The spirit indeed is willing, but the flesh is weak."

Philemon 1:14 ESV But I preferred to do nothing without your consent in order that your goodness might not be by compulsion but of your own accord.

Philippians 2:13 ESV For it is God who works in you, both to will and to work for his good pleasure.

Proverbs 3:5-6 ESV Trust in the Lord with all your heart, and do not lean on your own understanding. In all your ways acknowledge him, and he will make straight your paths.

Revelation 3:20 ESV Behold, I stand at the door and knock. If anyone hears my voice and opens the door, I will come in to him and eat with him, and he with me.

REINS

Use the skill of REINS to rein in your inaccurate, disproportionate or negativistic thoughts and help you take control of your mind (Houts, 2020).

R	Recognize the emotions or thoughts that are troubling you. Notice them without judgment. Naming them can also help shrink them to their proper proportion. Just noticing and naming your passing thoughts, feelings, and sensations can even provide some immediate relief.	Romans 12:12 ESV Rejoice in hope, be patient in tribulation, be constant in prayer. 2 Timothy 1:7 ESV For God gave us a spirit not of fear but of power and love and self-control.
E	Embrace gratitude. By embracing gratitude we can short circuit the fear we can feel when things are good and we experience joy. Unfortunately, at any moment our minds can begin creating a tragic mental drama from any vulnerability we may have. These narratives are often so powerful we feel it in our bodies usually via the vagus nerve which interfaces with the parasympathetic control of the heart, lungs, and digestive tract, making ourselves miserable in a tragedy that exists only in our mind. This foreboding can steal from our most prized moments.	1 Thessalonians 5:18 ESV Give thanks in all circumstances; for this is the will of God in Christ Jesus for you. 1 Thessalonians 5:16-18 ESV Rejoice always, pray without ceasing, give thanks in all circumstances; for this is the will of God in Christ Jesus for you.
I	Investigate and check for accuracy. Use your natural curiosity to delve more deeply into your distressing thoughts. Acknowledge them, look at them, sit with them, and ponder how they are attached to other thoughts. Consider: What triggered	Proverbs 11:3 ESV The integrity of the upright guides them, but the crookedness of the treacherous destroys them. Deuteronomy 25:15 ESV A full and fair weight you shall have, a full and fair

this thought? When have I felt this way before? What thoughts, feelings, and sensations are connected to this? Check the thought; is it accurate, realistic, and proportional? Would I apply this same standard to someone else I love? If the thought is accurate, realistic, proportional go with it; if it is not identify the facts that do not support it and make appropriate adjustments in your thinking.

measure you shall have, that your days may be long in the land that the LORD your God is giving you.

N   Notice but do not identify with your thoughts. Your painful thoughts, feelings, and sensations are not you. It has been estimated that the average person has between 12,000 and 60,000 thoughts per day. A vast majority can be negative and as many can be the same repetitive thoughts as the day before. Instead of identifying with your thoughts, you can allow them to come and go like the clouds in the sky. Noticing them as a natural function of your brain but not all necessary to dwell on or treat as anything other than simply a passing thought.

Romans 8:28 ESV And we know that for those who love God all things work together for good, for those who are called according to his purpose.

S   Self-compassion. Self-compassion means offering yourself consideration. It is the recognition and acceptance of your perfect imperfection and uniqueness. It is empathizing with yourself the way you might a friend or beloved other. By responding to the thought the way you would as if another person had said it to you. Maybe it is untrue, unkind or fault-finding. Stand up for yourself to encourage y bully voice to stop

Jeremiah 29:11-13 ESV For I know the plans I have for you, declares the LORD, plans for welfare and not for evil, to give you a future and a hope. Then you will call upon me and come and pray to me, and I will hear you. You will seek me and find me, when you seek me with all your heart.

1 Peter 3:8 ESV Finally, all of you, have unity of mind, sympathy, brotherly love, a tender heart, and a humble mind.

SCRAP it is a thought checking skill focused upon increasing clear thinking in Wise Mind. If your thinking is unreasonable or unrealistic in expectations, accuracy or out of proportion check it, challenge it and SCRAP it. Then focus on replacing it with the thinking that is specific in language, reasonable and realistic in expectations, accurate and proportional to the problem or situation (Houts, 2020).

S	Stop. Slow your thoughts to get a better look at them. Be specific.	Proverbs 4:23 ESV Keep your heart with all vigilance, for from it flow the springs of life.
		Ephesians 4:23 ESV And to be renewed in the spirit of your minds,
C	Check for thinking for details you may be overlooking or ignoring.	Proverbs 18:15 An intelligent heart acquires knowledge, and the ear of the wise seeks knowledge.
		Proverbs 2:6 ESV For the LORD gives wisdom; from his mouth come knowledge and understanding;
		Proverbs 12:1 ESV Whoever loves discipline loves knowledge, but he who hates reproof is stupid.
R	Realistic expectations of self, others in the situation?	Romans 15:7 ESV Therefore welcome one another as Christ has welcomed you, for the glory of God.
		Romans 3:23 ESV For all have sinned and fall short of the glory of God,
A	Accurate. Thinking, labels and language, nonjudgmentally.	John 17:17 ESV Sanctify them in the truth; your word is truth.
		Matthew 7:1-29 ESV "Judge not, that you be not judged. For with the judgment you pronounce you will be judged, and with the measure you use it will be measured to you. Why do you see the speck that is in your brother's eye, but do not notice the log that is

in your own eye? Or how can you say to your
brother, 'Let me take the speck out of your eye,'
when there is the log in your own eye? You
hypocrite, first take the log out of your own eye, and
then you will see clearly to take the speck out of your
brother's eye. ...

P	Proportional. Equal sized reaction to the size of the problem.	Ecclesiastes 7:9 ESV Be not quick in your spirit to become angry, for anger lodges in the heart of fools.

James 1:19-20 ESV Know this, my beloved brothers: let every person be quick to hear, slow to speak, slow to anger; for the anger of man does not produce the righteousness of God.

James 3:17 ESV But the wisdom from above is first pure, then peaceable, gentle, open to reason, full of mercy and good fruits, impartial and sincere.

Proverbs 10:19 ESV When words are many, transgression is not lacking, but whoever restrains his lips is prudent.

Proverbs 12:16 ESV The vexation of a fool is known at once, but the prudent ignores an insult.

Proverbs 14:29 ESV Whoever is slow to anger has great understanding, but he who has a hasty temper exalts folly.

Proverbs 15:1 ESV A soft answer turns away wrath, but a harsh word stirs up anger.

Proverbs 17:27-28 ESV Whoever restrains his words has knowledge, and he who has a cool spirit is a man of understanding. Even a fool who keeps silent is

considered wise; when he closes his lips, he is
deemed intelligent.

Proverbs 18:13 ESV If one gives an answer before he
hears, it is his folly and shame.

Proverbs 19:11 ESV Good sense makes one slow to
anger, and it is his glory to overlook an offense.

Proverbs 25:15 ESV With patience a ruler may be
persuaded, and a soft tongue will break a bone.

Proverbs 29:11 ESV A fool gives full vent to his
spirit, but a wise man quietly holds it back.

Hope

Deuteronomy 31:6 ESV Be strong and courageous. Do not fear or be in dread of them, for it is the LORD your God who goes with you. He will not leave you or forsake you."

Isaiah 40:31 ESV But they who wait for the LORD shall renew their strength; they shall mount up with wings like eagles; they shall run and not be weary; they shall walk and not faint.

Isaiah 41:10 ESV Fear not, for I am with you; be not dismayed, for I am your God; I will strengthen you, I will help you, I will uphold you with my righteous right hand.

Isaiah 61:1 ESV The Spirit of the Lord GOD is upon me, because the LORD has anointed me to bring good news to the poor; he has sent me to bind up the brokenhearted, to proclaim liberty to the captives, and the opening of the prison to those who are bound;

Jeremiah 29:11 ESV For I know the plans I have for you, declares the LORD, plans for welfare and not for evil, to give you a future and a hope.

Matthew 25:21 ESV His master said to him, 'Well done, good and faithful servant. You have been faithful over a little; I will set you over much. Enter into the joy of your master.'

Proverbs 24:14 ESV Know that wisdom is such to your soul; if you find it, there will be a future, and your hope will not be cut off.

Psalm 119:114 ESV You are my hiding place and my shield; I hope in your word.

Psalm 119:81 ESV My soul longs for your salvation; I hope in your word.

Psalm 130:1-135:21 ESV A Song of Ascents. Out of the depths I cry to you, O LORD! O Lord, hear my voice! Let your ears be attentive to the voice of my pleas for mercy! If you, O LORD, should mark iniquities, O Lord, who could stand? But with you there is forgiveness, that you may be feared. I wait for the LORD, my soul waits, and in his word I hope; ...

Psalm 130:5 ESV I wait for the LORD, my soul waits, and in his word I hope;

Psalm 130:7 ESV O Israel, hope in the LORD! For with the LORD there is steadfast love, and with him is plentiful redemption.

Psalm 146:5 ESV Blessed is he whose help is the God of Jacob, whose hope is in the LORD his God,

Psalm 147:11 ESV But the LORD takes pleasure in those who fear him, in those who hope in his steadfast love.

Psalm 25:2 ESV O my God, in you I trust; let me not be put to shame; let not my enemies exult over me.

Psalm 25:5 ESV Lead me in your truth and teach me, for you are the God of my salvation; for you I wait all the day long.

Psalm 31:2 ESV Incline your ear to me; rescue me speedily! Be a rock of refuge for me, a strong fortress to save me!

Psalm 31:24 ESV Be strong, and let your heart take courage, all you who wait for the LORD!

Psalm 33:18 ESV Behold, the eye of the LORD is on those who fear him, on those who hope in his steadfast love,

Psalm 33:22 ESV Let your steadfast love, O LORD, be upon us, even as we hope in you.

Psalm 39:7 ESV "And now, O Lord, for what do I wait? My hope is in you.

Psalm 42:11 ESV Why are you cast down, O my soul, and why are you in turmoil within me? Hope in God; for I shall again praise him, my salvation and my God.

Psalm 43:5 ESV Why are you cast down, O my soul, and why are you in turmoil within me? Hope in God; for I shall again praise him, my salvation and my God.

Psalm 62:5 ESV For God alone, O my soul, wait in silence, for my hope is from him.

Psalm 71:14 ESV But I will hope continually and will praise you yet more and more.

Psalm 71:5 ESV For you, O Lord, are my hope, my trust, O LORD, from my youth.

Colossians 3:1-2 ESV If then you have been raised with Christ, seek the things that are above, where Christ is, seated at the right hand of God. Set your minds on things that are above, not on things that are on earth.

Isaiah 43:1-2 ESV But now thus says the LORD, he who created you, O Jacob, he who formed you, O Israel: "Fear not, for I have redeemed you; I have called you by name, you are mine. When you pass through the waters, I will be with you; and through the rivers, they shall not overwhelm you; when you walk through fire you shall not be burned, and the flame shall not consume you.

Titus 1:1-2 ESV Paul, a servant of God and an apostle of Jesus Christ, for the sake of the faith of God's elect and their knowledge of the truth, which accords with godliness, in hope of eternal life, which God, who never lies, promised before the ages began

Hebrews 11:1-3 ESV Now faith is the assurance of things hoped for, the conviction of things not seen. For by it the people of old received their commendation. By faith we understand that the universe was created by the word of God, so that what is seen was not made out of things that are visible.

1 Timothy 1:1 ESV Paul, an apostle of Christ Jesus by command of God our Savior and of Christ Jesus our hope,

1 Peter 1:2 ESV According to the foreknowledge of God the Father, in the sanctification of the Spirit, for obedience to Jesus Christ and for sprinkling with his blood: May grace and peace be multiplied to you.

Titus 1:2 ESV In hope of eternal life, which God, who never lies, promised before the ages began

1 Peter 1:3 ESV Blessed be the God and Father of our Lord Jesus Christ! According to his great mercy, he has caused us to be born again to a living hope through the resurrection of Jesus Christ from the dead,

1 Thessalonians 1:3 ESV Remembering before our God and Father your work of faith and labor of love and steadfastness of hope in our Lord Jesus Christ.

Philippians 1:6 ESV And I am sure of this, that he who began a good work in you will bring it to completion at the day of Jesus Christ.

2 Timothy 1:7 ESV For God gave us a spirit not of fear but of power and love and self-control.

1 Peter 1:13 ESV Therefore, preparing your minds for action, and being sober-minded, set your hope fully on the grace that will be brought to you at the revelation of Jesus Christ.

Ephesians 1:18 ESV Having the eyes of your hearts enlightened, that you may know what is the hope to which he has called you, what are the riches of his glorious inheritance in the saints,

1 Peter 1:21 ESV Who through him are believers in God, who raised him from the dead and gave him glory, so that your faith and hope are in God.

Colossians 1:27 ESV To them God chose to make known how great among the Gentiles are the riches of the glory of this mystery, which is Christ in you, the hope of glory.

1 Corinthians 2:9 ESV But, as it is written, "What no eye has seen, nor ear heard, nor the heart of man imagined, what God has prepared for those who love him"—

Titus 2:13 ESV Waiting for our blessed hope, the appearing of the glory of our great God and Savior Jesus Christ,

1 John 3:3 ESV And everyone who thus hopes in him purifies himself as he is pure.

1 Peter 3:3 ESV Do not let your adorning be external—the braiding of hair and the putting on of gold jewelry, or the clothing you wear—

Hebrews 3:6 ESV But Christ is faithful over God's house as a son. And we are his house, if indeed we hold fast our confidence and our boasting in our hope.

Titus 3:7 ESV So that being justified by his grace we might become heirs according to the hope of eternal life.

2 Corinthians 3:12 ESV Since we have such a hope, we are very bold,

Philippians 3:13-14 ESV Brothers, I do not consider that I have made it my own. But one thing I do: forgetting what lies behind and straining forward to what lies ahead, I press on toward the goal for the prize of the upward call of God in Christ Jesus.

1 Peter 3:15 ESV But in your hearts honor Christ the Lord as holy, always being prepared to make a defense to anyone who asks you for a reason for the hope that is in you; yet do it with gentleness and respect,

Joel 3:16 ESV The LORD roars from Zion, and utters his voice from Jerusalem, and the heavens and the earth quake. But the LORD is a refuge to his people, a stronghold to the people of Israel.

John 3:16 ESV "For God so loved the world, that he gave his only Son, that whoever believes in him should not perish but have eternal life.

Zephaniah 3:17 ESV The LORD your God is in your midst, a mighty one who will save; he will rejoice over you with gladness; he will quiet you by his love; he will exult over you with loud singing.

Lamentations 3:24 ESV "The LORD is my portion," says my soul, "therefore I will hope in him."

Ephesians 4:4 ESV There is one body and one Spirit—just as you were called to the one hope that belongs to your call—

1 Thessalonians 4:13 ESV But we do not want you to be uninformed, brothers, about those who are asleep, that you may not grieve as others do who have no hope.

2 Corinthians 4:16-18 ESV So we do not lose heart. Though our outer self is wasting away, our inner self is being renewed day by day. For this light momentary affliction is preparing for us an eternal weight of glory beyond all comparison, as we look not to the things that are seen but to the things that are unseen. For the things that are seen are transient, but the things that are unseen are eternal.

2 Corinthians 4:17-18 ESV For this light momentary affliction is preparing for us an eternal weight of glory beyond all comparison, as we look not to the things that are seen

but to the things that are unseen. For the things that are seen are transient, but the things that are unseen are eternal.

Romans 5:2 ESV Through him we have also obtained access by faith into this grace in which we stand, and we rejoice in hope of the glory of God.

Galatians 5:5 ESV For through the Spirit, by faith, we ourselves eagerly wait for the hope of righteousness.

Romans 5:5 ESV And hope does not put us to shame, because God's love has been poured into our hearts through the Holy Spirit who has been given to us.

1 Thessalonians 5:8 ESV But since we belong to the day, let us be sober, having put on the breastplate of faith and love, and for a helmet the hope of salvation.

1 Peter 5:10 ESV And after you have suffered a little while, the God of all grace, who has called you to his eternal glory in Christ, will himself restore, confirm, strengthen, and establish you.

Galatians 6:8 ESV For the one who sows to his own flesh will from the flesh reap corruption, but the one who sows to the Spirit will from the Spirit reap eternal life.

1 Timothy 6:17 ESV As for the rich in this present age, charge them not to be haughty, nor to set their hopes on the uncertainty of riches, but on God, who richly provides us with everything to enjoy.

Hebrews 6:18-19 ESV So that by two unchangeable things, in which it is impossible for God to lie, we who have fled for refuge might have strong encouragement to hold fast to the hope set before us. We have this as a sure and steadfast anchor of the soul, a hope that enters into the inner place behind the curtain,

Hebrews 6:19 ESV We have this as a sure and steadfast anchor of the soul, a hope that enters into the inner place behind the curtain,

Micah 7:7 ESV But as for me, I will look to the LORD; I will wait for the God of my salvation; my God will hear me.

Romans 8:2 ESV For the law of the Spirit of life has set you free in Christ Jesus from the law of sin and death.

Romans 8:18 ESV For I consider that the sufferings of this present time are not worth comparing with the glory that is to be revealed to us.

Romans 8:24 ESV For in this hope we were saved. Now hope that is seen is not hope. For who hopes for what he sees?

Romans 8:24-25 ESV For in this hope we were saved. Now hope that is seen is not hope. For who hopes for what he sees? But if we hope for what we do not see, we wait for it with patience.

Romans 8:25 ESV But if we hope for what we do not see, we wait for it with patience.

Romans 8:28 ESV And we know that for those who love God all things work together for good, for those who are called according to his purpose.

Psalm 9:18 ESV For the needy shall not always be forgotten, and the hope of the poor shall not perish forever.

Mark 9:23 ESV And Jesus said to him, "'If you can'! All things are possible for one who believes."

Psalm 10:17 ESV O LORD, you hear the desire of the afflicted; you will strengthen their heart; you will incline your ear

Hebrews 10:23 ESV Let us hold fast the confession of our hope without wavering, for he who promised is faithful.

Hebrews 11:1 ESV Now faith is the assurance of things hoped for, the conviction of things not seen.

Job 11:18 ESV And you will feel secure, because there is hope; you will look around and take your rest in security.

Matthew 11:28 ESV Come to me, all who labor and are heavy laden, and I will give you rest.

Romans 12:12 ESV Rejoice in hope, be patient in tribulation, be constant in prayer.

Proverbs 13:2 ESV From the fruit of his mouth a man eats what is good, but the desire of the treacherous is for violence.

Proverbs 13:12 ESV Hope deferred makes the heart sick, but a desire fulfilled is a tree of life.

1 Corinthians 13:13 ESV So now faith, hope, and love abide, these three; but the greatest of these is love.

Job 13:15 ESV Though he slay me, I will hope in him; yet I will argue my ways to his face.

Romans 15:4 ESV For whatever was written in former days was written for our instruction, that through endurance and through the encouragement of the Scriptures we might have hope.

Romans 15:13 ESV May the God of hope fill you with all joy and peace in believing, so that by the power of the Holy Spirit you may abound in hope.

1 Corinthians 15:19 ESV If in Christ we have hope in this life only, we are of all people most to be pitied.

Psalm 16:9 ESV Therefore my heart is glad, and my whole being rejoices; my flesh also dwells secure.

Jeremiah 17:7 ESV "Blessed is the man who trusts in the LORD, whose trust is the LORD.

Revelation 21:4 ESV He will wipe away every tear from their eyes, and death shall be no more, neither shall there be mourning, nor crying, nor pain anymore, for the former things have passed away."

Proverbs 23:18 ESV Surely there is a future, and your hope will not be cut off.

1 Corinthians 13:1-13 ESV If I speak in the tongues of men and of angels, but have not love, I am a noisy gong or a clanging cymbal. And if I have prophetic powers, and understand all mysteries and all knowledge, and if I have all faith, so as to remove mountains, but have not love, I am nothing. If I give away all I have, and if I deliver up my body to be burned, but have not love, I gain nothing. Love is patient and kind; love does not envy or boast; it is not arrogant or rude. It does not insist on its own way; it is not irritable or resentful; ...

Proverbs 10:1-28:28 ESV The proverbs of Solomon. A wise son makes a glad father, but a foolish son is a sorrow to his mother. Treasures gained by wickedness do not profit, but righteousness delivers from death. The LORD does not let the righteous go hungry, but he thwarts the craving of the wicked. A slack hand causes poverty, but the hand of the diligent makes rich. He who gathers in summer is a prudent son, but he who sleeps in harvest is a son who brings shame. ...

Romans 5:2-5 ESV Through him we have also obtained access by faith into this grace in which we stand, and we rejoice in hope of the glory of God. Not only that, but we rejoice in our sufferings, knowing that suffering produces endurance, and endurance produces character, and character produces hope, and hope does not put us to shame, because God's love has been poured into our hearts through the Holy Spirit who has been given to us.

Romans 5:3-4 ESV Not only that, but we rejoice in our sufferings, knowing that suffering produces endurance, and endurance produces character, and character produces hope,

Jeremiah 17:7-8 ESV "Blessed is the man who trusts in the LORD, whose trust is the LORD. He is like a tree planted by water, that sends out its roots by the stream, and does not fear when heat comes, for its leaves remain green, and is not anxious in the year of drought, for it does not cease to bear fruit."

Psalm 121:7-8 ESV The LORD will keep you from all evil; he will keep your life. The LORD will keep your going out and your coming in from this time forth and forevermore.

Psalm 62:5-6 KJV My soul, wait thou only upon God; for my expectation is from him. He only is my rock and my salvation: he is my defence; I shall not be moved.

Isaiah 43:2 KJV When thou passest through the waters, I will be with thee; and through the rivers, they shall not overflow thee: when thou walkest through the fire, thou shalt not be burned; neither shall the flame kindle upon thee.

Matthew 17:20 KJV And Jesus said unto them, Because of your unbelief: for verily I say unto you, If ye have faith as a grain of mustard seed, ye shall say unto this mountain, Remove hence to yonder place; and it shall remove; and nothing shall be impossible unto you.

Matthew 28:20 KJV Teaching them to observe all things whatsoever I have commanded you: and, lo, I am with you always, even unto the end of the world. Amen.

2 Corinthians 5:7 KJV we walk by faith, not by sight:

1 Corinthians 15:10 KJV But by the grace of God I am what I am: and his grace which was bestowed upon me was not in vain; but I laboured more abundantly than they all: yet not I, but the grace of God which was with me.

Matthew 19:26 KJV But Jesus beheld them, and said unto them, With men this is impossible; but with God all things are possible.

Psalms 5:12 KJV For thou, LORD, wilt bless the righteous; with favour wilt thou compass him as with a shield.

Philippians 3:13 NIV Brothers and sisters, I do not consider myself yet to have taken hold of it. But one thing I do: Forgetting what is behind and straining toward what is ahead,

Isaiah 43:5 NIV Do not be afraid, for I am with you; I will bring your children from the east and gather you from the west.

Matthew 5:16 NIV In the same way, let your light shine before others, that they may see your good deeds and glorify your Father in heaven.

Matthew 28:20 NIV and teaching them to obey everything I have commanded you. And surely I am with you always, to the very end of the age.

1 John 4:16 KJV And we have known and believed the love that God hath to us. God is love; and he that dwelleth in love dwelleth in God, and God in him.

Psalm 23 KJV The LORD is my shepherd; I shall not want. He maketh me to lie down in green pastures: he leadeth me beside the still waters. He restoreth my soul: he leadeth me in the paths of righteousness for his name's sake. Yea, though I walk through the valley of the shadow of death, I will fear no evil: for thou art with me; thy rod and thy staff they comfort me. Thou preparest a table before me in the presence of mine enemies: thou anointest my head with oil; my cup runneth over. Surely goodness and mercy shall follow me all the days of my life: and I will dwell in the house of the LORD forever.

Luke 12:22-26 KJV And he said unto his disciples, Therefore I say unto you, Take no thought for your life, what ye shall eat; neither for the body, what ye shall put on. The life is more than meat, and the body is more than raiment. Consider the ravens: for they neither sow nor reap; which neither have storehouse nor barn; and God feedeth them: how much more are ye better than the fowls? And which of you with taking thought can add to his stature one cubit? If ye then be not able to do that thing which is least, why take ye thought for the rest?

Helplessness

Genesis 29:23-26 ESV But in the evening he took his daughter Leah and brought her to Jacob, and he went in to her. (Laban gave his female servant Zilpah to his daughter Leah to be her servant.) And in the morning, behold, it was Leah! And Jacob said to Laban, "What is this you have done to me? Did I not serve with you for Rachel? Why then have you deceived me?" Laban said, "It is not so done in our country, to give the younger before the firstborn.

Isaiah 29:20-22 ESV For the ruthless shall come to nothing and the scoffer cease, and all who watch to do evil shall be cut off, who by a word make a man out to be an offender, and lay a snare for him who reproves in the gate, and with an empty plea turn aside him who is in the right. Therefore thus says the Lord, who redeemed Abraham, concerning the house of Jacob: "Jacob shall no more be ashamed, no more shall his face grow pale.

Isaiah 49:14-16 ESV But Zion said, "The Lord has forsaken me; my Lord has forgotten me." "Can a woman forget her nursing child, that she should have no compassion on the son of her womb? Even these may forget, yet I will not forget you. Behold, I have engraved you on the palms of my hands; your walls are continually before me.

Isaiah 53:6 ESV All we like sheep have gone astray; we have turned—every one—to his own way; and the Lord has laid on him the iniquity of us all.

Isaiah 54:17 ESV No weapon that is fashioned against you shall succeed, and you shall refute every tongue that rises against you in judgment. This is the heritage of the servants of the Lord and their vindication from me, declares the Lord."

Isaiah 59:21 ESV And as for me, this is my covenant with them," says the Lord: "My Spirit that is upon you, and my words that I have put in your mouth, shall not depart out of your mouth, or out of the mouth of your offspring, or out of the mouth of your children's offspring," says the Lord, "from this time forth and forevermore."

Jeremiah 50:33-35 ESV "Thus says the Lord of hosts: The people of Israel are oppressed, and the people of Judah with them. All who took them captive have held them fast; they refuse to let them go. Their Redeemer is strong; the Lord of hosts is his name. He will surely plead their cause, that he may give rest to the earth, but unrest to the inhabitants of Babylon. "A sword against the Chaldeans, declares the Lord, and against the inhabitants of Babylon, and against her officials and her wise men!

Matthew 26:51-54 ESV And behold, one of those who were with Jesus stretched out his hand and drew his sword and struck the servant of the high priest and cut off his ear. Then Jesus said to him, "Put your sword back into its place. For all who take the sword will perish by the sword. Do you think that I cannot appeal to my Father, and he will at once send me more than twelve legions of angels? But how then should the Scriptures be fulfilled, that it must be so?"

Proverbs 29:25 ESV The fear of man lays a snare, but whoever trusts in the Lord is safe.

Psalm 35:10 ESV All my bones shall say, "O Lord, who is like you, delivering the poor from him who is too strong for him, the poor and needy from him who robs him?"

Psalm 54:4 ESV Behold, God is my helper; the Lord is the upholder of my life.

Psalm 23:1-6 ESV A Psalm of David. The Lord is my shepherd; I shall not want. He makes me lie down in green pastures. He leads me beside still waters. He restores my soul. He leads me in paths of righteousness for his name's sake. Even though I walk through the valley of the shadow of death, I will fear no evil, for you are with me; your rod and your staff, they comfort me. You prepare a table before me in the presence of my enemies; you anoint my head with oil; my cup overflows. ...

Acts 1:8 ESV But you will receive power when the Holy Spirit has come upon you, and you will be my witnesses in Jerusalem and in all Judea and Samaria, and to the end of the earth."

Job 1:13-20 ESV Now there was a day when his sons and daughters were eating and drinking wine in their oldest brother's house, and there came a messenger to Job and said, "The oxen were plowing and the donkeys feeding beside them, and the Sabeans fell upon them and took them and struck down the servants with the edge of the sword, and I alone have escaped to tell you." While he was yet speaking, there came another and said, "The fire of God fell from heaven and burned up the sheep and the servants and consumed them, and I alone have escaped to tell you." While he was yet speaking, there came another and said, "The Chaldeans formed three groups and made a raid on the camels and took them and struck down the servants with the edge of the sword, and I alone have escaped to tell you." ...

Genesis 1:28 ESV And God blessed them. And God said to them, "Be fruitful and multiply and fill the earth and subdue it, and have dominion over the fish of the sea and over the birds of the heavens and over every living thing that moves on the earth."

1 John 2:1 ESV My little children, I am writing these things to you so that you may not sin. But if anyone does sin, we have an advocate with the Father, Jesus Christ the righteous.

Job 2:7 ESV So Satan went out from the presence of the Lord and struck Job with loathsome sores from the sole of his foot to the crown of his head.

Hebrews 2:17-18 ESV Therefore he had to be made like his brothers in every respect, so that he might become a merciful and faithful high priest in the service of God, to make propitiation for the sins of the people. For because he himself has suffered when tempted, he is able to help those who are being tempted.

Acts 2:23 ESV This Jesus, delivered up according to the definite plan and foreknowledge of God, you crucified and killed by the hands of lawless men.

Proverbs 3:5 ESV Trust in the Lord with all your heart, and do not lean on your own understanding.

Colossians 3:17 ESV And whatever you do, in word or deed, do everything in the name of the Lord Jesus, giving thanks to God the Father through him.

John 3:17-19 ESV For God did not send his Son into the world to condemn the world, but in order that the world might be saved through him. Whoever believes in him is not condemned, but whoever does not believe is condemned already, because he has not believed in the name of the only Son of God. And this is the judgment: the light has come into the world, and people loved the darkness rather than the light because their works were evil.

Romans 3:22-24 ESV The righteousness of God through faith in Jesus Christ for all who believe. For there is no distinction: for all have sinned and fall short of the glory of God, and are justified by his grace as a gift, through the redemption that is in Christ Jesus,

Hebrews 4:15 ESV For we do not have a high priest who is unable to sympathize with our weaknesses, but one who in every respect has been tempted as we are, yet without sin.

Ephesians 4:17-19 ESV Now this I say and testify in the Lord, that you must no longer walk as the Gentiles do, in the futility of their minds. They are darkened in their understanding, alienated from the life of God because of the ignorance that is in them, due to their hardness of heart. They have become callous and have given themselves up to sensuality, greedy to practice every kind of impurity.

Acts 5:4 ESV While it remained unsold, did it not remain your own? And after it was sold, was it not at your disposal? Why is it that you have contrived this deed in your heart? You have not lied to man but to God."

Romans 5:8 ESV But God shows his love for us in that while we were still sinners, Christ died for us.

Romans 5:12 ESV Therefore, just as sin came into the world through one man, and death through sin, and so death spread to all men because all sinned -

Romans 5:14 ESV Yet death reigned from Adam to Moses, even over those whose sinning was not like the transgression of Adam, who was a type of the one who was to come.

Galatians 5:16 ESV But I say, walk by the Spirit, and you will not gratify the desires of the flesh.

Mark 5:25-26 ESV And there was a woman who had had a discharge of blood for twelve years, and who had suffered much under many physicians, and had spent all that she had, and was no better but rather grew worse.

Mark 5:27-34 ESV She had heard the reports about Jesus and came up behind him in the crowd and touched his garment. For she said, "If I touch even his garments, I will be made well." And immediately the flow of blood dried up, and she felt in her body that she was healed of her disease. And Jesus, perceiving in himself that power had gone out from him, immediately turned about in the crowd and said, "Who touched my garments?" And his disciples said to him, "You see the crowd pressing around you, and yet you say, 'Who touched me?'" ...

Romans 6:23 ESV For the wages of sin is death, but the free gift of God is eternal life in Christ Jesus our Lord.

Luke 6:37 ESV Judge not, and you will not be judged; condemn not, and you will not be condemned; forgive, and you will be forgiven;

Mark 7:6 ESV And he said to them, "Well did Isaiah prophesy of you hypocrites, as it is written, "'This people honors me with their lips, but their heart is far from me;

Mark 7:9 And he said to them, "You have a fine way of rejecting the commandment of God in order to establish your tradition!

John 8:24 ESV I told you that you would die in your sins, for unless you believe that I am he you will die in your sins."

Romans 8:26-27 ESV Likewise the Spirit helps us in our weakness. For we do not know what to pray for as we ought, but the Spirit himself intercedes for us with groanings too deep for words. And he who searches hearts knows what is the mind of the Spirit, because the Spirit intercedes for the saints according to the will of God.

Romans 8:28 ESV And we know that for those who love God all things work together for good, for those who are called according to his purpose.

Romans 8:29 ESV For those whom he foreknew he also predestined to be conformed to the image of his Son, in order that he might be the firstborn among many brothers.

Romans 8:37-39 ESV No, in all these things we are more than conquerors through him who loved us. For I am sure that neither death nor life, nor angels nor rulers, nor things present nor things to come, nor powers, nor height nor depth, nor anything else in all creation, will be able to separate us from the love of God in Christ Jesus our Lord.

Matthew 9:16-17 ESV No one puts a piece of unshrunk cloth on an old garment, for the patch tears away from the garment, and a worse tear is made. Neither is new wine put into old wineskins. If it is, the skins burst and the wine is spilled and the skins are destroyed. But new wine is put into fresh wineskins, and so both are preserved."

1 Corinthians 10:13 ESV No temptation has overtaken you that is not common to man. God is faithful, and he will not let you be tempted beyond your ability, but with the temptation he will also provide the way of escape, that you may be able to endure it.

Psalm 10:13-15 ESV Why does the wicked renounce God and say in his heart, "You will not call to account"? But you do see, for you note mischief and vexation, that you may take it into your hands; to you the helpless commits himself; you have been the helper of the fatherless. Break the arm of the wicked and evildoer; call his wickedness to account till you find none.

Romans 10:13 ESV For "everyone who calls on the name of the Lord will be saved."

Matthew 10:18-20 ESV And you will be dragged before governors and kings for my sake, to bear witness before them and the Gentiles. When they deliver you over, do not be anxious how you are to speak or what you are to say, for what you are to say will be given to you in that hour. For it is not you who speak, but the Spirit of your Father speaking through you.

Mark 10:38-40 ESV Jesus said to them, "You do not know what you are asking. Are you able to drink the cup that I drink, or to be baptized with the baptism with which I am baptized?" And they said to him, "We are able." And Jesus said to them, "The cup that I drink you will drink, and with the baptism with which I am baptized, you will be baptized, but to sit at my right hand or at my left is not mine to grant, but it is for those for whom it has been prepared."

Mark 10:46-48 ESV And they came to Jericho. And as he was leaving Jericho with his disciples and a great crowd, Bartimaeus, a blind beggar, the son of Timaeus, was sitting by the roadside. And when he heard that it was Jesus of Nazareth, he began to cry out and say, "Jesus, Son of David, have mercy on me!" And many rebuked him, telling him to be silent. But he cried out all the more, "Son of David, have mercy on me!"

Matthew 11:19 ESV The Son of Man came eating and drinking, and they say, 'Look at him! A glutton and a drunkard, a friend of tax collectors and sinners!' Yet wisdom is justified by her deeds."

Mark 11:22-24 ESV And Jesus answered them, "Have faith in God. Truly, I say to you, whoever says to this mountain, 'Be taken up and thrown into the sea,' and does not doubt in his heart, but believes that what he says will come to pass, it will be done for him. Therefore I tell you, whatever you ask in prayer, believe that you have received it, and it will be yours.

Mark 11:24 ESV Therefore I tell you, whatever you ask in prayer, believe that you have received it, and it will be yours.

Mark 11:25 ESV And whenever you stand praying, forgive, if you have anything against anyone, so that your Father also who is in heaven may forgive you your trespasses."

Daniel 12:2 ESV And many of those who sleep in the dust of the earth shall awake, some to everlasting life, and some to shame and everlasting contempt.

Mark 12:30 ESV And you shall love the Lord your God with all your heart and with all your soul and with all your mind and with all your strength.'

Mark 12:40 ESV Who devour widows' houses and for a pretense make long prayers. They will receive the greater condemnation."

John 14:6 ESV Jesus said to him, "I am the way, and the truth, and the life. No one comes to the Father except through me.

Mark 14:24 ESV And he said to them, "This is my blood of the covenant, which is poured out for many.

Mark 14:36 ESV And he said, "Abba, Father, all things are possible for you. Remove this cup from me. Yet not what I will, but what you will."

John 15:5 ESV I am the vine; you are the branches. Whoever abides in me and I in him, he it is that bears much fruit, for apart from me you can do nothing.

Acts 16:31 ESV And they said, "Believe in the Lord Jesus, and you will be saved, you and your household."

John 17:5 ESV And now, Father, glorify me in your own presence with the glory that I had with you before the world existed.

Acts 17:30 ESV The times of ignorance God overlooked, but now he commands all people everywhere to repent,

Luke 18:13-14 ESV But the tax collector, standing far off, would not even lift up his eyes to heaven, but beat his breast, saying, 'God, be merciful to me, a sinner!' I tell you, this man went down to his house justified, rather than the other. For everyone who exalts himself will be humbled, but the one who humbles himself will be exalted."

Luke 18:19 ESV And Jesus said to him, "Why do you call me good? No one is good except God alone.

Matthew 19:14-15 ESV But Jesus said, "Let the little children come to me and do not hinder them, for to such belongs the kingdom of heaven." And he laid his hands on them and went away.

Job 19:25-26 ESV For I know that my Redeemer lives, and at the last he will stand upon the earth. And after my skin has been thus destroyed, yet in my flesh I shall see God,

Genesis 21:14-21 ESV So Abraham rose early in the morning and took bread and a skin of water and gave it to Hagar, putting it on her shoulder, along with the child, and sent her away. And she departed and wandered in the wilderness of Beersheba. When the water in the skin was gone, she put the child under one of the bushes. Then she went and sat down opposite him a good way off, about the distance of a bowshot, for she said, "Let me not look on the death of the child." And as she sat opposite him, she lifted up her voice and wept. And God heard the voice of the boy, and the angel of God called to Hagar from heaven and said to her, "What troubles you, Hagar? Fear not, for God has heard the voice of the boy where he is. Up! Lift up the boy, and hold him fast with your hand, for I will make him into a great nation." ...

Luke 23:34 ESV And Jesus said, "Father, forgive them, for they know not what they do." And they cast lots to divide his garments.

Luke 23:40-43 ESV But the other rebuked him, saying, "Do you not fear God, since you are under the same sentence of condemnation? And we indeed justly, for we are receiving the due reward of our deeds; but this man has done nothing wrong." And he said, "Jesus, remember me when you come into your kingdom." And he said to him, "Truly, I say to you, today you will be with me in paradise."

Psalm 2:1-12 ESV Why do the nations rage and the peoples plot in vain? The kings of the earth set themselves, and the rulers take counsel together, against the Lord and against his Anointed, saying, "Let us burst their bonds apart and cast away their cords from us." He who sits in the heavens laughs; the Lord holds them in derision. Then he will speak to them in his wrath, and terrify them in his fury, saying, ...

Colossians 1:1-29 ESV Paul, an apostle of Christ Jesus by the will of God, and Timothy our brother, To the saints and faithful brothers in Christ at Colossae: Grace to you and peace from God our Father. We always thank God, the Father of our Lord Jesus Christ, when we pray for you, since we heard of your faith in Christ Jesus and of the love that you have for all the saints, because of the hope laid up for you in heaven. Of this you have heard before in the word of the truth, the gospel, ...

Hebrews 12:2-3 ESV Looking to Jesus, the founder and perfecter of our faith, who for the joy that was set before him endured the cross, despising the shame, and is seated at the right hand of the throne of God. Consider him who endured from sinners such hostility against himself, so that you may not grow weary or fainthearted.

Luke 18:2-8 ESV He said, "In a certain city there was a judge who neither feared God nor respected man. And there was a widow in that city who kept coming to him and saying, 'Give me justice against my adversary.' For a while he refused, but afterward he said to himself, 'Though I neither fear God nor respect man, yet because this widow keeps bothering me, I will give her justice, so that she will not beat me down by her continual coming.'" And the Lord said, "Hear what the unrighteous judge says. ...

Mark 5:2-8 ESV And when Jesus had stepped out of the boat, immediately there met him out of the tombs a man with an unclean spirit. He lived among the tombs. And no one could bind him anymore, not even with a chain, for he had often been bound with shackles and chains, but he wrenched the chains apart, and he broke the shackles in pieces. No one had the strength to subdue him. Night and day among the tombs and on the mountains he was always crying out and cutting himself with stones. And when he saw Jesus from afar, he ran and fell down before him.

Psalm 61:3-4 ESV For you have been my refuge, a strong tower against the enemy. Let me dwell in your tent forever! Let me take refuge under the shelter of your wings! Selah

Romans 8:3-4 ESV For God has done what the law, weakened by the flesh, could not do. By sending his own Son in the likeness of sinful flesh and for sin, he condemned sin in the flesh, in order that the righteous requirement of the law might be fulfilled in us, who walk not according to the flesh but according to the Spirit.

Ephesians 2:3-5 ESV Among whom we all once lived in the passions of our flesh, carrying out the desires of the body and the mind, and were by nature children of wrath, like the rest of mankind. But God, being rich in mercy, because of the great love with which he loved us, even when we were dead in our trespasses, made us alive together with Christ—by grace you have been saved -

John 8:3-5 ESV The scribes and the Pharisees brought a woman who had been caught in adultery, and placing her in the midst they said to him, "Teacher, this woman has been caught in the act of adultery. Now in the Law, Moses commanded us to stone such women. So what do you say?"

Deuteronomy 31:5-6 ESV And the Lord will give them over to you, and you shall do to them according to the whole commandment that I have commanded you. Be strong and courageous. Do not fear or be in dread of them, for it is the Lord your God who goes with you. He will not leave you or forsake you."

Psalm 1:5-6 ESV Therefore the wicked will not stand in the judgment, nor sinners in the congregation of the righteous; for the Lord knows the way of the righteous, but the way of the wicked will perish.

Romans 5:5-7 ESV And hope does not put us to shame, because God's love has been poured into our hearts through the Holy Spirit who has been given to us. For while we were still weak, at the right time Christ died for the ungodly. For one will scarcely die for a righteous person—though perhaps for a good person one would dare even to die -

Philippians 2:6-7 ESV Who, though he was in the form of God, did not count equality with God a thing to be grasped, but emptied himself, by taking the form of a servant, being born in the likeness of men.

Genesis 16:6-11 ESV But Abram said to Sarai, "Behold, your servant is in your power; do to her as you please." Then Sarai dealt harshly with her, and she fled from her. The angel of the Lord found her by a spring of water in the wilderness, the spring on the way to Shur. And he said, "Hagar, servant of Sarai, where have you come from and where are you going?" She said, "I am fleeing from my mistress Sarai." The angel of the Lord said to her, "Return to your mistress and submit to her." The angel of the Lord also said to her, "I will surely multiply your offspring so that they cannot be numbered for multitude." ...

Revelation 21:7-8 ESV The one who conquers will have this heritage, and I will be his God and he will be my son. But as for the cowardly, the faithless, the detestable, as for murderers, the sexually immoral, sorcerers, idolaters, and all liars, their portion will be in the lake that burns with fire and sulfur, which is the second death."

Jeremiah 33:7-9 ESV I will restore the fortunes of Judah and the fortunes of Israel, and rebuild them as they were at first. I will cleanse them from all the guilt of their sin against me, and I will forgive all the guilt of their sin and rebellion against me. And this city shall be to me a name of joy, a praise and a glory before all the nations of the earth who shall hear of all the good that I do for them. They shall fear and tremble because of all the good and all the prosperity I provide for it.

Isaiah 40:10-11 ESV Behold, the Lord God comes with might, and his arm rules for him; behold, his reward is with him, and his recompense before him. He will tend his flock like a shepherd; he will gather the lambs in his arms; he will carry them in his bosom, and gently lead those that are with young.

Romans 2:11-13 ESV For God shows no partiality. For all who have sinned without the law will also perish without the law, and all who have sinned under the law will be judged by the law. For it is not the hearers of the law who are righteous before God, but the doers of the law who will be justified.

Matthew 18:12-14 ESV What do you think? If a man has a hundred sheep, and one of them has gone astray, does he not leave the ninety-nine on the mountains and go in search of the one that went astray? And if he finds it, truly, I say to you, he rejoices over it more than over the ninety-nine that never went astray. So it is not the will of my Father who is in heaven that one of these little ones should perish.

Proverbs 6:12-15 ESV A worthless person, a wicked man, goes about with crooked speech, winks with his eyes, signals with his feet, points with his finger, with perverted heart devises evil, continually sowing discord; therefore calamity will come upon him suddenly; in a moment he will be broken beyond healing.

Chapter 2

Distress Tolerance

Distress Tolerance

1 Corinthians 4:5 ESV Therefore do not pronounce judgment before the time, before the Lord comes, who will bring to light the things now hidden in darkness and will disclose the purposes of the heart. Then each one will receive his commendation from God.

1 Corinthians 6:19-20 ESV Or do you not know that your body is a temple of the Holy Spirit within you, whom you have from God? You are not your own, for you were bought with a price. So glorify God in your body.

1 Corinthians 7:26 ESV I think that in view of the present distress it is good for a person to remain as he is.

1 Peter 4:13 ESV But rejoice insofar as you share Christ's sufferings, that you may also rejoice and be glad when his glory is revealed.

1 Thessalonians 4:16 ESV For the Lord himself will descend from heaven with a cry of command, with the voice of an archangel, and with the sound of the trumpet of God. And the dead in Christ will rise first.

Acts 2:38 ESV And Peter said to them, "Repent and be baptized every one of you in the name of Jesus Christ for the forgiveness of your sins, and you will receive the gift of the Holy Spirit.

Acts 2:44 ESV And all who believed were together and had all things in common.

Amos 3:7 ESV "For the Lord GOD does nothing without revealing his secret to his servants the prophets.

Ecclesiastes 6:3 ESV If a man fathers a hundred children and lives many years, so that the days of his years are many, but his soul is not satisfied with life's good things, and he also has no burial, I say that a stillborn child is better off than he.

Ephesians 5:18 ESV And do not get drunk with wine, for that is debauchery, but be filled with the Spirit,

Hebrews 9:28 ESV So Christ, having been offered once to bear the sins of many, will appear a second time, not to deal with sin but to save those who are eagerly waiting for him.

Isaiah 16:10 ESV And joy and gladness are taken away from the fruitful field, and in the vineyards no songs are sung, no cheers are raised; no treader treads out wine in the presses; I have put an end to the shouting.

Isaiah 25:9 ESV It will be said on that day, "Behold, this is our God; we have waited for him, that he might save us. This is the LORD; we have waited for him; let us be glad and rejoice in his salvation."

Isaiah 41:17 ESV When the poor and needy seek water, and there is none, and their tongue is parched with thirst, I the LORD will answer them; I the God of Israel will not forsake them.

John 3:16-17 ESV "For God so loved the world, that he gave his only Son, that whoever believes in him should not perish but have eternal life. For God did not send his Son into the world to condemn the world, but in order that the world might be saved through him.

John 6:27 ESV Do not work for the food that perishes, but for the food that endures to eternal life, which the Son of Man will give to you. For on him God the Father has set his seal."

Luke 12:33 ESV Sell your possessions, and give to the needy. Provide yourselves with moneybags that do not grow old, with a treasure in the heavens that does not fail, where no thief approaches and no moth destroys.

Luke 21:34-36 ESV "But watch yourselves lest your hearts be weighed down with dissipation and drunkenness and cares of this life, and that day come upon you suddenly like a trap. For it will come upon all who dwell on the face of the whole earth. But stay awake at all times, praying that you may have strength to escape all these things that are going to take place, and to stand before the Son of Man."

Luke 3:11 ESV And he answered them, "Whoever has two tunics is to share with him who has none, and whoever has food is to do likewise."

Luke 3:21 ESV Now when all the people were baptized, and when Jesus also had been baptized and was praying, the heavens were opened,

Luke 4:1-13 ESV And Jesus, full of the Holy Spirit, returned from the Jordan and was led by the Spirit in the wilderness for forty days, being tempted by the devil. And he ate nothing during those days. And when they were ended, he was hungry. The devil said to him, "If you are the Son of God, command this stone to become bread." And Jesus answered him, "It is written, 'Man shall not live by bread alone.'" And the devil took him up and showed him all the kingdoms of the world in a moment of time, ...

Luke 6:20-21 ESV And he lifted up his eyes on his disciples, and said: "Blessed are you who are poor, for yours is the kingdom of God. "Blessed are you who are hungry now, for you shall be satisfied. "Blessed are you who weep now, for you shall laugh.

Luke 9:26 ESV For whoever is ashamed of me and of my words, of him will the Son of Man be ashamed when he comes in his glory and the glory of the Father and of the holy angels.

Mark 16:1 ESV When the Sabbath was past, Mary Magdalene, Mary the mother of James, and Salome bought spices, so that they might go and anoint him.

Mark 9:43 ESV And if your hand causes you to sin, cut it off. It is better for you to enter life crippled than with two hands to go to hell, to the unquenchable fire.

Matthew 24:14 ESV And this gospel of the kingdom will be proclaimed throughout the whole world as a testimony to all nations, and then the end will come.

Matthew 24:1-51 ESV Jesus left the temple and was going away, when his disciples came to point out to him the buildings of the temple. But he answered them, "You see all these, do you not? Truly, I say to you, there will not be left here one stone upon another that will not be thrown down." As he sat on the Mount of Olives, the disciples came to him privately, saying, "Tell us, when will these things be, and what will be the sign of your coming and of the end of the age?" And Jesus answered them, "See that no one leads you astray. For many will come in my name, saying, 'I am the Christ,' and they will lead many astray. ...

Matthew 26:24 ESV The Son of Man goes as it is written of him, but woe to that man by whom the Son of Man is betrayed! It would have been better for that man if he had not been born."

Matthew 28:19 ESV Go therefore and make disciples of all nations, baptizing them in the name of the Father and of the Son and of the Holy Spirit,

Matthew 6:24 ESV "No one can serve two masters, for either he will hate the one and love the other, or he will be devoted to the one and despise the other. You cannot serve God and money.

Philippians 3:21 ESV Who will transform our lowly body to be like his glorious body, by the power that enables him even to subject all things to himself.

Proverbs 20:1 ESV Wine is a mocker, strong drink a brawler, and whoever is led astray by it is not wise.

Proverbs 23:20 ESV Be not among drunkards or among gluttonous eaters of meat,

Proverbs 23:29-35 ESV Who has woe? Who has sorrow? Who has strife? Who has complaining? Who has wounds without cause? Who has redness of eyes? Those who tarry long over wine; those who go to try mixed wine. Do not look at wine when it is red, when it sparkles in the cup and goes down smoothly. In the end it bites like a serpent and stings like an adder. Your eyes will see strange things, and your heart utter perverse things. ...

Psalm 104:15 ESV And wine to gladden the heart of man, oil to make his face shine and bread to strengthen man's heart.

Psalm 110:1 ESV A Psalm of David. The LORD says to my Lord: "Sit at my right hand, until I make your enemies your footstool."

Psalm 139:14 ESV I praise you, for I am fearfully and wonderfully made. Wonderful are your works; my soul knows it very well.

Psalm 4:7 ESV You have put more joy in my heart than they have when their grain and wine abound.

Psalm 86:7 ESV In the day of my trouble I call upon you, for you answer me.

Titus 2:13 ESV Waiting for our blessed hope, the appearing of the glory of our great God and Savior Jesus Christ,

Titus 2:3 ESV Older women likewise are to be reverent in behavior, not slanderers or slaves to much wine. They are to teach what is good,

Zechariah 10:7 ESV Then Ephraim shall become like a mighty warrior, and their hearts shall be glad as with wine. Their children shall see it and be glad; their hearts shall rejoice in the LORD.

IMPROVE is a distress tolerance skill to use to for reducing emotional intensity and increase management of stressful situations (Houts, 2020).

I	Imagery	Hebrews 11:1 ESV Now faith is the assurance of things hoped for, the conviction of things not seen.
M	Meaning	Hebrews 4:12 ESV For the word of God is living and active, sharper than any two-edged sword, piercing to the division of soul and of spirit, of joints and of marrow, and discerning the thoughts and intentions of the heart.
P	Prayer	John 16:33 ESV I have said these things to you, that in me you may have peace. In the world you will have tribulation. But take heart; I have overcome the world."
		James 1:5 ESV If any of you lacks wisdom, let him ask God, who gives generously to all without reproach, and it will be given him.
		1 Thessalonians 5:17-18 ESV Pray without ceasing, give thanks in all circumstances; for this is the will of God in Christ Jesus for you.
R	Relaxation	Philippians 4:6-7 ESV Do not be anxious about anything, but in everything by prayer and supplication with thanksgiving let your requests be made known to God. And the peace of God, which surpasses all understanding, will guard your hearts and your minds in Christ Jesus.
		John 14:27 ESV Peace I leave with you; my peace I give to you. Not as the world gives do I give to you. Let not your hearts be troubled, neither let them be afraid.
		Psalm 46:10 ESV "Be still, and know that I am God. I will be exalted among the nations, I will be exalted in the earth!"
		Matthew 6:33 ESV But seek first the kingdom of God and his righteousness, and all these things will be added to you.

Matthew 11:28-30 ESV Come to me, all who labor and are heavy laden, and I will give you rest. Take my yoke upon you, and learn from me, for I am gentle and lowly in heart, and you will find rest for your souls. For my yoke is easy, and my burden is light."

Psalm 4:8 ESV In peace I will both lie down and sleep; for you alone, O LORD, make me dwell in safety.

O	One thing at a time	Matthew 6:34 ESV "Therefore do not be anxious about tomorrow, for tomorrow will be anxious for itself. Sufficient for the day is its own trouble.
V	Vacation	Proverbs 4:23 ESV Keep your heart with all vigilance, for from it flow the springs of life.
E	Encouragement	2 Corinthians 4:18 ESV As we look not to the things that are seen but to the things that are unseen. For the things that are seen are transient, but the things that are unseen are eternal.

TIPP is a distress tolerance skill used to reduce emotional intensity by down regulating the nervous system acronym for Temperature, Intense Exercise, Paced Breathing, and Paired Muscle Relaxation (Linehan, 2014).

T	Temperature	Romans 12:2 ESV Do not be conformed to this world, but be transformed by the renewal of your mind, that by testing you may discern what is the will of God, what is good and acceptable and perfect.
I	Intense Exercise	Titus 2:12 ESV Training us to renounce ungodliness and worldly passions, and to live self-controlled, upright, and godly lives in the present age,
P	Paced Breathing	1 Thessalonians 5:8 ESV But since we belong to the day, let us be sober, having put on the breastplate of faith and love, and for a helmet the hope of salvation.
P	Paired Muscle Relaxation	Ephesians 6:11 ESV Put on the whole armor of God, that you may be able to stand against the schemes of the devil.
		1 Peter 5:7 ESV Casting all your anxieties on him, because he cares for you.

BARK

BARK is used to reduce emotional intensity and serves to protect delicate inner tissue from external damage increasing distress tolerance in harsh environments; to make progress rely on your BARK (Houts, 2020).

B   Be present. Do not miss your life simply because this moment is hard, and you wish for it to be different. Be mindful and open to the moment as it is. Take what it has to bring you and allow it to fall away as it came. Is it a lesson? A blessing? Both? Be persistent. The difference between success and failure is how many times you try. Try; try again, because practice makes progress. Competence and ability come with practice. The fact is that to be successful, efficient, or effective at something, you must invest the time to get there. There is no substitute for practice.

Matthew 6:34 ESV Therefore do not be anxious about tomorrow, for tomorrow will be anxious for itself. Sufficient for the day is its own trouble.

Isaiah 43:18-19 ESV Remember not the former things, nor consider the things of old. Behold, I am doing a new thing; now it springs forth, do you not perceive it? I will make a way in the wilderness and rivers in the desert.

Jeremiah 29:11 ESV For I know the plans I have for you, declares the Lord, plans for welfare and not for evil, to give you a future and a hope.

Ephesians 5:15-16 ESV Look carefully then how you walk, not as unwise but as wise, making the best use of the time, because the days are evil.

Romans 12:2 ESV Do not be conformed to this world, but be transformed by the renewal of your mind, that by testing you may discern what is the will of God, what is good and acceptable and perfect.

A   Accept that which you cannot change. Do not waste any of

your limited resources on things such as how your parents raised

1 Thessalonians 5:21 ESV But test everything; hold fast what is good.

Romans 8:28 ESV And we know that for those who love God all things work together for

you, the past, things beyond your control, wishes that did not come true, or how your story is taken a turn that you did not plan for. Acceptance and change are your options. If it will not be changed in this moment, your only other option is acceptance.

good, for those who are called according to his purpose.

John 6:37 ESV All that the Father gives me will come to me, and whoever comes to me I will never cast out.

Galatians 5:1 ESV For freedom Christ has set us free; stand firm therefore, and do not submit again to a yoke of slavery.

R Recognize that your ability to change is far greater than what you believe. You cannot change the rules of the universe, your height, your nose, or numerous other things in your daily life. You can however, change how hard you work, how grateful you are for your blessings, how you approach the things in your life that you do not care for or prefer, how open you are to new ideas, how you approach challenges and difficulties, and how willing you are to invest persistent effort in the direction of what you want.

Joshua 1:9 ESV Have I not commanded you? Be strong and courageous. Do not be frightened, and do not be dismayed, for the LORD your God is with you wherever you go."

Jeremiah 29:11 ESV For I know the plans I have for you, declares the LORD, plans for welfare and not for evil, to give you a future and a hope.

Ecclesiastes 3:1 ESV For everything there is a season, and a time for every matter under heaven:

Proverbs 18:15 ESV An intelligent heart acquires knowledge, and the ear of the wise seeks knowledge.

K Know when assistance is required. Remember to balance the dialectic of independence and support. It is a fallacy to think that anyone in this life succeeds of absolutely his or her own volition, effort, and talent. It simply is not true.

John 14:13-14 ESV Whatever you ask in my name, this I will do, that the Father may be glorified in the Son. If you ask me anything in my name, I will do it.

Psalm 121:2 ESV My help comes from the Lord, who made heaven and earth.

Matthew 7:7 ESV "Ask, and it will be given to you; seek, and you will find; knock, and it will be opened to you.

Philippians 4:13 ESV I can do all things through him who strengthens me.

Matthew 11:28 ESV Come to me, all who labor and are heavy laden, and I will give you rest.

BRACES

BRACES is a distress tolerance skill for managing uncomfortable social events (Houts, 2020).

B	Be in the moment. Breath.	Job 33:4 ESV The Spirit of God has made me, and the breath of the Almighty gives me life.
R	Relax your body.	John 14:27 ESV Peace I leave with you; my peace I give to you. Not as the world gives do I give to you. Let not your hearts be troubled, neither let them be afraid.
A	Attitude of willingness, soft accepting, and positivity. Act as if you are comfortable and happy to be there.	Isaiah 1:19 ESV if you are willing and obedient, you shall eat the good of the land;
C	Casual conversation, if appropriate. Avoid religion, politics, private information, wound sharing, cursing, withdrawing, wall hugging, or isolating.	Hebrews 10:24 ESV And let us consider how to stir up one another to love and good works, Ephesians 4:2 ESV With all humility and gentleness, with patience, bearing with one another in love,
E	Eye contact, if appropriate. Act as if you are enjoying the event, follow the action. Try to match the intensity of the activity. Participate.	Matthew 28:19 Go therefore and make disciples of all nations, baptizing them in the name of the Father and of the Son and of the Holy Spirit,
S	Soft smile. Speak when spoken to. Select someone you have met and visit, or would like to meet and introduce yourself.	Romans 12:18 ESV If possible, so far as it depends on you, live peaceably with all.

GLAD PACK

GLAD PACK is a distress tolerance skill-focused upon making progress by practicing being pleased in our ability to carry ourselves towards progress (Houts, 2020).

G	Goal: Be effective towards goal, be intentional. Grit: Action despite fear or discomfort.	Proverbs 16:3 ESV Commit your work to the LORD, and your plans will be established.
L	Label mindfully specifically, accurately, and proportionally. List any steps to be taken in order and revise as necessary. Take only one step at a time.	John 8:32 ESV And you will know the truth, and the truth will set you free.
A	Accept change and standstill as a natural part of life. Wait for time to unfold. Wait for opportunities for the impossible to become possible.	Galatians 6:9 ESV And let us not grow weary of doing good, for in due season we will reap, if we do not give up.
D	Determined: Skillful effort balanced with patient tolerance and persistence, willingness, and rest.	Isaiah 1:19 ESV If you are willing and obedient, you shall eat the good of the land;
		2 Corinthians 8:12 ESV For if the readiness is there, it is acceptable according to what a person has, not according to what he does not have.
		Proverbs 3:5-6 ESV Trust in the Lord with all your heart, and do not lean on your own understanding. In all your ways acknowledge him, and he will make straight your paths.

P	Progress, not perfection.	Psalm 119:96 NIV To all perfection I see a limit, but your commands are boundless.
A	Act intentionally, mindfully in clear thinking, proportionally, taking only one step at a time. When there is nothing to do at this moment, allow the moment to pass in calm without rumination.	Colossians 3:23 ESV Whatever you do, work heartily, as for the Lord and not for men,
C	Commitment: Renew as needed, goal-focused, the big picture, doing only that which is necessary and appropriate.	Proverbs 16:3 ESV Commit your work to the LORD, and your plans will be established. Psalm 37:5 ESV Commit your way to the LORD; trust in him, and he will act. 1 Kings 8:61 ESV Let your heart therefore be wholly true to the LORD our God, walking in his statutes and keeping his commandments, as at this day."
K	Kind: Always loving kindness to self and others in thoughts, words, and actions. Do not burn bridges unless you are in a Wise Mind, and that is your clear thinking intention.	Ephesians 4:32 ESV Be kind to one another, tenderhearted, forgiving one another, as God in Christ forgave you.

BIRD CAGE

BIRD CAGE is a burning bridge harm reduction distress tolerance and relapse prevention skill focused upon proactively breaking down and removing supports for problem addictive behaviors. Bridge burning acknowledges that relapse of problem behaviors occurs easily when the supporting structures and constituents of the problem behavior continue to exist in easy access. Using the term bird cage as an internally controlled air traffic space wherein purposefully created structure and support increases safety by controlling entry and preventing problematic intrusion (Houts, 2020).

B	Block all problem behavior related contacts. Build new habits to replace old problem patterns.	1 Corinthians 15:33 ESV Do not be deceived: "Bad company ruins good morals."
I	Insert barriers to your problem behavior for situations that are likely to arise.	Proverbs 4:14-15 ESV Do not enter the path of the wicked, and do not walk in the way of the evil. Avoid it; do not go on it; turn away from it and pass on. Proverbs 13:20 ESV Whoever walks with the wise becomes wise, but the companion of fools will suffer harm.
R	Remove the means of acting on harmful urges and behaviors from easy access your home, bedroom, social environment, and workspace.	1 Thessalonians 5:22 ESV Abstain from every form of evil. Ephesians 5:11 ESV Take no part in the unfruitful works of darkness, but instead expose them.
D	Delete all problem behavior related contacts from your telephone. Do not carry cash. Do not go off your schedule. Dedicate planned scheduled time for healthy variation and novelty.	Proverbs 13:20 ESV Whoever walks with the wise becomes wise, but the companion of fools will suffer harm.
C	Challenge go-ahead thoughts every time they arise. Commit to be honest with yourself and	1 Peter 5:8 ESV Be sober-minded; be watchful. Your adversary the devil prowls

	others about all parts of the problem behavior.	around like a roaring lion, seeking someone to devour.
A	Actively avoid obtaining objects, paraphernalia, situations, and localities related to the problem behavior. Actively and consistently, engage healthy supports. G Go to a safe place before engaging in the problem behavior.	1 Thessalonians 5:22 ESV Abstain from every form of evil. Ephesians 5:11 ESV Take no part in the unfruitful works of darkness, but instead expose them.
G	Goal: unhealthy behavior extinction and maintaining that extinction.	Romans 12:2 ESV Do not be conformed to this world, but be transformed by the renewal of your mind, that by testing you may discern what is the will of God, what is good and acceptable and perfect. Psalm 101:3-4 ESV I will not set before my eyes anything that is worthless. I hate the work of those who fall away; it shall not cling to me. A perverse heart shall be far from me; I will know nothing of evil.
E	Environmental management- actively and daily.	1 Thessalonians 5:22 ESV Abstain from every form of evil. Ephesians 5:11 ESV Take no part in the unfruitful works of darkness, but instead expose them. 1 Peter 5:8 ESV Be sober-minded; be watchful. Your adversary the devil prowls around like a roaring lion, seeking someone to devour.

Chapter 3

Emotion Regulation

Emotion Regulation

1 Corinthians 13:13 ESV So now faith, hope, and love abide, these three; but the greatest of these is love.

1 Peter 3:18 ESV For Christ also suffered once for sins, the righteous for the unrighteous, that he might bring us to God, being put to death in the flesh but made alive in the spirit,

1 Peter 4:8 ESV Above all, keep loving one another earnestly, since love covers a multitude of sins.

Acts 2:38 ESV And Peter said to them, "Repent and be baptized every one of you in the name of Jesus Christ for the forgiveness of your sins, and you will receive the gift of the Holy Spirit.

Colossians 2:8 ESV See to it that no one takes you captive by philosophy and empty deceit, according to human tradition, according to the elemental spirits of the world, and not according to Christ.

Ecclesiastes 9:10 ESV Whatever your hand finds to do, do it with your might, for there is no work or thought or knowledge or wisdom in Sheol, to which you are going.

Ephesians 6:13 ESV Therefore take up the whole armor of God, that you may be able to withstand in the evil day, and having done all, to stand firm.

John 4:24 ESV God is spirit, and those who worship him must worship in spirit and truth."

Matthew 10:28 ESV And do not fear those who kill the body but cannot kill the soul. Rather fear him who can destroy both soul and body in hell.

Matthew 5:28 ESV But I say to you that everyone who looks at a woman with lustful intent has already committed adultery with her in his heart.

Matthew 7:1-2 ESV "Judge not, that you be not judged. For with the judgment you pronounce you will be judged, and with the measure you use it will be measured to you.

Philippians 4:13 ESV I can do all things through him who strengthens me.

Philippians 4:6-7 ESV Do not be anxious about anything, but in everything by prayer and supplication with thanksgiving let your requests be made known to God. And the peace of God, which surpasses all understanding, will guard your hearts and your minds in Christ Jesus.

Proverbs 29:11 ESV A fool gives full vent to his spirit, but a wise man quietly holds it back.

Psalm 4:8 ESV In peace I will both lie down and sleep; for you alone, O Lord, make me dwell in safety.

Psalm 6:5 ESV For in death there is no remembrance of you; in Sheol who will give you praise?

Romans 12:11 ESV Do not be slothful in zeal, be fervent in spirit, serve the Lord.

Romans 12:15 ESV Rejoice with those who rejoice, weep with those who weep.

Romans 12:2 ESV Do not be conformed to this world, but be transformed by the renewal of your mind, that by testing you may discern what is the will of God, what is good and acceptable and perfect.

3R's

3R's is an emotional regulation skill for use with anxiety and fear responses that are out of proportion.

R	Recognize the anxiety	2 Timothy 1:7 ESV For God gave us a spirit not of fear but of power and love and self-control. 1 Peter 5:6-7 ESV Humble yourselves, therefore, under the mighty hand of God so that at the proper time he may exalt you, casting all your anxieties on him, because he cares for you.
R	Relax your body	Philippians 4:6-7 ESV Do not be anxious about anything, but in everything by prayer and supplication with thanksgiving let your requests be made known to God. And the peace of God, which surpasses all understanding, will guard your hearts and your minds in Christ Jesus.
R	Redirect the energy to something productive	John 14:27 ESV Peace I leave with you; my peace I give to you. Not as the world gives do I give to you. Let not your hearts be troubled, neither let them be afraid. Joshua 1:9 ESV Have I not commanded you? Be strong and courageous. Do not be frightened, and do not be dismayed, for the LORD your God is with you wherever you go."

BELOVEDS

BELOVEDS is an emotional regulation self-respect building skill. Practice making small changed to increase self-respect (Houts, 2020).

B	Be your own best friend.	Proverbs 4:23 ESV Keep your heart with all vigilance, for from it flow the springs of life.
		Haggai 1:5 ESV Now, therefore, thus says the Lord of hosts: Consider your ways.
		Psalm 139:23 ESV Search me, O God, and know my heart! Try me and know my thoughts!
E	Expect perfectly imperfect from self and others.	Romans 3:23 ESV For all have sinned and fall short of the glory of God,
		Jude 1:24 ESV Now to him who is able to keep you from stumbling and to present you blameless before the presence of his glory with great joy,
		1 Peter 3:9 ESV Do not repay evil for evil or reviling for reviling, but on the contrary, bless, for to this you were called, that you may obtain a blessing.
L	Leave out problematic evaluations.	Luke 6:37 ESV "Judge not, and you will not be judged; condemn not, and you will not be condemned; forgive, and you will be forgiven;
		Romans 2:1 ESV Therefore you have no excuse, O man, every one of you who judges. For in passing judgment on another you condemn yourself, because you, the judge, practice the very same things.
O	Openness. Express genuinely who you are as a unique	2 Timothy 2:15 ESV Do your best to present yourself to God as one approved, a worker who

individual. Be mindful of masking, going along or other behaviors that result in guilt, shame, anger or self-disgust.

has no need to be ashamed, rightly handling the word of truth.

James 5:16 ESV Therefore, confess your sins to one another and pray for one another, that you may be healed. The prayer of a righteous person has great power as it is working.

Colossians 3:9 ESV Do not lie to one another, seeing that you have put off the old self with its practices

Proverbs 12:22 ESV Lying lips are an abomination to the Lord, but those who act faithfully are his delight.

V   Values; act in ways that allows you to feel moral.

Philippians 4:8 ESV Finally, brothers, whatever is true, whatever is honorable, whatever is just, whatever is pure, whatever is lovely, whatever is commendable, if there is any excellence, if there is anything worthy of praise, think about these things.

Galatians 5:22-23 ESV But the fruit of the Spirit is love, joy, peace, patience, kindness, goodness, faithfulness, gentleness, self-control; against such things there is no law.

Matthew 6:24 ESV "No one can serve two masters, for either he will hate the one and love the other, or he will be devoted to the one and despise the other. You cannot serve God and money.

E   Express your wants and needs, likes and dislikes gently and genuinely.

Colossians 3:9-10 ESV Do not lie to one another, seeing that you have put off the old self with its practices and have put on the new self, which is being renewed in knowledge after the image of its creator.

D	Do only what works. S Set healthy boundaries. Say yes, no or maybe. When appropriate and you actually mean it. Be honest, it saves time. Saying no to others is often saying yes to yourself.	Colossians 3:23-24 ESV Whatever you do, work heartily, as for the Lord and not for men, knowing that from the Lord you will receive the inheritance as your reward. You are serving the Lord Christ.

Proverbs 14:23 ESV In all toil there is profit, but mere talk tends only to poverty.

Philippians 4:13 ESV I can do all things through him who strengthens me. |
| S | Self-care; care for yourself like you are someone you love and value. Say so, when someone mistreats you speak up and say that you will not accept being mistreated and if it continues you will have to make a change. | 1 Corinthians 6:19-20 ESV Or do you not know that your body is a temple of the Holy Spirit within you, whom you have from God? You are not your own, for you were bought with a price. So glorify God in your body.

1 Corinthians 3:16 ESV Do you not know that you are God's temple and that God's Spirit dwells in you?

3 John 1:2 ESV Beloved, I pray that all may go well with you and that you may be in good health, as it goes well with your soul. |

ATTRACTS is an emotion regulation skill focused on seeking helpful social supports to avoid harmful behaviors (Houts, 2020).

A	Actively avoid situations and localities related to the problem behavior. Delete all problem behavior related contacts from your telephone. Do not go off your established routine. Block all problem behavior related contacts on social media. Build new habits.	1 Corinthians 15:33 ESV Do not be deceived: "Bad company ruins good morals."
T	Talk to a safe person before engaging in the problem behavior	Proverbs 3:5-6 ESV Trust in the Lord with all your heart, and do not lean on your own understanding. In all your ways acknowledge him, and he will make straight your paths.
T	Tell others when you are feeling unsafe.	Proverbs 11:14 ESV Where there is no guidance, a people falls, but in an abundance of counselors there is safety.
R	Remove the means of acting on urges from easy access.	Galatians 6:7-8 ESV Do not be deceived: God is not mocked, for whatever one sows, that will he also reap. For the one who sows to his own flesh will from the flesh reap corruption, but the one who sows to the Spirit will from the Spirit reap eternal life.
A	Actively engage healthy supports.	James 1:5 ESV If any of you lacks wisdom, let him ask God, who gives generously to all without reproach, and it will be given him.
C	Challenge 'go-ahead' thoughts about the problem behavior.	1 Corinthians 10:13 ESV No temptation has overtaken you that is not common to man. God is faithful, and he will not let you be tempted beyond your ability, but with the temptation he will also provide the way of escape, that you may be able to endure it.

T	Take a break. Use a waiting period every single urge.	James 4:7 ESV Submit yourselves therefore to God. Resist the devil, and he will flee from you.
S	Go to a Safe Place before engaging in the problem behavior.	1 Corinthians 10:13 ESV No temptation has overtaken you that is not common to man. God is faithful, and he will not let you be tempted beyond your ability, but with the temptation he will also provide the way of escape, that you may be able to endure it.

Build MASTERy

Build MASTERy is an emotional regulation skill (Linehan, 2014).

| M | Mindful to emotions | Proverbs 4:23 ESV Keep your heart with all vigilance, for from it flow the springs of life.

Galatians 5:22-23 ESV But the fruit of the Spirit is love, joy, peace, patience, kindness, goodness, faithfulness, gentleness, self-control; against such things there is no law.

Philippians 4:6-7 ESV Do not be anxious about anything, but in everything by prayer and supplication with thanksgiving let your requests be made known to God. And the peace of God, which surpasses all understanding, will guard your hearts and your minds in Christ Jesus.

Psalm 42:5 ESV Why are you cast down, O my soul, and why are you in turmoil within me? Hope in God; for I shall again praise him, my salvation |

| A | Act opposite to emotion | Ephesians 4:26-27 ESV Be angry and do not sin; do not let the sun go down on your anger, and give no opportunity to the devil. |

| S | Self-validation | Colossians 3:2 ESV Set your minds on things that are above, not on things that are on earth. |

| T | Turn the mind | Romans 12:2 ESV Do not be conformed to this world, but be transformed by the renewal of your mind, that by testing you may discern what is the will of God, what is good and acceptable and perfect.

2 Corinthians 10:5 ESV We destroy arguments and every lofty opinion raised against the knowledge of God, and take every thought captive to obey Christ, |

Philippians 4:8 ESV Finally, brothers, whatever is true, whatever is honorable, whatever is just, whatever is pure, whatever is lovely, whatever is commendable, if there is any excellence, if there is anything worthy of praise, think about these things.

Colossians 3:2 ESV Set your minds on things that are above, not on things that are on earth.

Ephesians 4:23 ESV And to be renewed in the spirit of your minds,

E	Experience building positive	Galatians 6:9 ESV And let us not grow weary of doing good, for in due season we will reap, if we do not give up.

2 Thessalonians 3:13 ESV As for you, brothers, do not grow weary in doing good.

Ephesians 2:10 ESV For we are his workmanship, created in Christ Jesus for good works, which God prepared beforehand, that we should walk in them.

Psalm 37:3 ESV Trust in the LORD, and do good; dwell in the land and befriend faithfulness.

Colossians 3:23 ESV Whatever you do, work heartily, as for the Lord and not for men,

R	Radical Acceptance	Philippians 4:8 ESV Finally, brothers, whatever is true, whatever is honorable, whatever is just, whatever is pure, whatever is lovely, whatever is commendable, if there is any excellence, if there is anything worthy of praise, think about these things.

Job 38:36 ESV Who has put wisdom in the inward parts or given understanding to the mind?

Hebrews 11:1 ESV Now faith is the assurance of things hoped for, the conviction of things not seen.

1 Thessalonians 5:21 ESV But test everything; hold fast what is good.

Romans 8:28 ESV And we know that for those who love God all things work together for good, for those who are called according to his purpose.

y

| Build positive experiences | Hebrews 4:12 ESV For the word of God is living and active, sharper than any two-edged sword, piercing to the division of soul and of spirit, of joints and of marrow, and discerning the thoughts and intentions of the heart. |
| | |

Build positive experiences

Hebrews 4:12 ESV For the word of God is living and active, sharper than any two-edged sword, piercing to the division of soul and of spirit, of joints and of marrow, and discerning the thoughts and intentions of the heart.

1 Corinthians 4:5 ESV Therefore do not pronounce judgment before the time, before the Lord comes, who will bring to light the things now hidden in darkness and will disclose the purposes of the heart. Then each one will receive his commendation from God.

Romans 12:2 ESV Do not be conformed to this world, but be transformed by the renewal of your mind, that by testing you may discern what is the will of God, what is good and acceptable and perfect.

Be mindful of current emotion

2 Timothy 1:7 ESV For God gave us a spirit not of fear but of power and love and self-control.

Colossians 3:8 ESV But now you must put them all away: anger, wrath, malice, slander, and obscene talk from your mouth.

Colossians 3:2 ESV Set your minds on things that are above, not on things that are on earth.

Opposite to emotion action

Philippians 4:13 ESV I can do all things through him who strengthens me.

1 Corinthians 13:13 ESV So now faith, hope, and love abide, these three; but the greatest of these is love.

Romans 8:28 ESV And we know that for those who love God all things work together for good, for those who are called according to his purpose.

John 14:26 ESV But the Helper, the Holy Spirit, whom the Father will send in my name, he will teach

you all things and bring to your remembrance all that
I have said to you.

Isaiah 40:31 ESV But they who wait for
the LORD shall renew their strength; they shall mount
up with wings like eagles; they shall run and not be
weary; they shall walk and not faint.

Proverbs 3:5 ESV Trust in the LORD with all your
heart, and do not lean on your own understanding.

Psalm 139:14 ESV I praise you, for I am fearfully
and wonderfully made. Wonderful are your works;
my soul knows it very well.

TEASED

An emotion regulation reducing vulnerability skill (Houts, 2020).

| T | Treat physical illness | James 5:14 ESV Is anyone among you sick? Let him call for the elders of the church, and let them pray over him, anointing him with oil in the name of the Lord.

Proverbs 1:5-6 ESV Let the wise hear and increase in learning, and the one who understands obtain guidance, to understand a proverb and a saying, the words of the wise and their riddles. 3 helpful votes Helpful Not Helpful

When the Spirit of truth comes, he will guide you into all the truth, for he will not speak on his own authority, but whatever he hears he will speak, and he will declare to you the things that are to come. |

| E | Eating | Genesis 9:3 ESV Every moving thing that lives shall be food for you. And as I gave you the green plants, I give you everything. |

| A | Altering drugs | Proverbs 20:1 ESV Wine is a mocker, strong drink a brawler, and whoever is led astray by it is not wise.

Ephesians 5:18 ESV And do not get drunk with wine, for that is debauchery, but be filled with the Spirit,

Galatians 5:21 ESV Envy, drunkenness, orgies, and things like these. I warn you, as I warned you before, that those who do such things will not inherit the kingdom of God.

Romans 13:13 ESV Let us walk properly as in the daytime, not in orgies and drunkenness, not in sexual immorality and sensuality, not in quarreling and jealousy.

1 Peter 5:8 ESV Be sober-minded; be watchful. Your adversary the devil prowls around like a roaring lion, seeking someone to devour.

2 Timothy 1:7 ESV For God gave us a spirit not of fear but of power and love and self-control. |

S   Sleep   Proverbs 3:24 ESV If you lie down, you will not be afraid;
                          when you lie down, your sleep will be sweet.

                          Psalm 4:8 ESV In peace I will both lie down and sleep; for
                          you alone, O LORD, make me dwell in safety.

                          Psalm 3:5 ESV I lay down and slept; I woke again, for
                          the LORD sustained me.

E   Exercise   1 Timothy 4:8 ESV For while bodily training is of some
                          value, godliness is of value in every way, as it holds
                          promise for the present life and also for the life to come.

                          1 Corinthians 6:19-20 ESV Or do you not know that your
                          body is a temple of the Holy Spirit within you, whom you
                          have from God? You are not your own, for you were bought
                          with a price. So glorify God in your body.

                          Proverbs 31:17 ESV She dresses herself with strength and
                          makes her arms strong.

D   Daily   Luke 11:3 ESV Give us each day our daily bread,

                          Psalm 68:19 ESV Blessed be the Lord, who daily bears us
                          up; God is our salvation.

Chapter 4

Interpersonal Effectiveness

1 Corinthians 13:13 ESV So now faith, hope, and love abide, these three; but the greatest of these is love.

1 Corinthians 13:4-7 ESV Love is patient and kind; love does not envy or boast; it is not arrogant or rude. It does not insist on its own way; it is not irritable or resentful; it does not rejoice at wrongdoing, but rejoices with the truth. Love bears all things, believes all things, hopes all things, endures all things.

1 Corinthians 15:33 ESV Do not be deceived: "Bad company ruins good morals."

1 Corinthians 16:14 ESV Let all that you do be done in love.

1 Corinthians 6:18 ESV Flee from sexual immorality. Every other sin a person commits is outside the body, but the sexually immoral person sins against his own body.

1 Corinthians 7:2 ESV But because of the temptation to sexual immorality, each man should have his own wife and each woman her own husband.

1 Corinthians 7:9 ESV But if they cannot exercise self-control, they should marry. For it is better to marry than to burn with passion.

1 John 3:1 ESV See what kind of love the Father has given to us, that we should be called children of God; and so we are. The reason why the world does not know us is that it did not know him.

1 John 4:7 ESV Beloved, let us love one another, for love is from God, and whoever loves has been born of God and knows God.

1 Peter 1:3 ESV Blessed be the God and Father of our Lord Jesus Christ! According to his great mercy, he has caused us to be born again to a living hope through the resurrection of Jesus Christ from the dead,

1 Peter 1:3-5 ESV Blessed be the God and Father of our Lord Jesus Christ! According to his great mercy, he has caused us to be born again to a living hope through the resurrection of Jesus Christ from the dead, to an inheritance that is imperishable, undefiled, and unfading, kept in heaven for you, who by God's power are being guarded through faith for a salvation ready to be revealed in the last time.

1 Peter 3:7 ESV Likewise, husbands, live with your wives in an understanding way, showing honor to the woman as the weaker vessel, since they are heirs with you of the grace of life, so that your prayers may not be hindered.

1 Peter 4:8 ESV Above all, keep loving one another earnestly, since love covers a multitude of sins.

1 Peter 5:6-7 ESV Humble yourselves, therefore, under the mighty hand of God so that at the proper time he may exalt you, casting all your anxieties on him, because he cares for you.

1 Thessalonians 3:12 ESV And may the Lord make you increase and abound in love for one another and for all, as we do for you,

1 Thessalonians 5:11 ESV Therefore encourage one another and build one another up, just as you are doing.

1 Timothy 5:8 ESV But if anyone does not provide for his relatives, and especially for members of his household, he has denied the faith and is worse than an unbeliever.

2 Corinthians 5:17 ESV Therefore, if anyone is in Christ, he is a new creation. The old has passed away; behold, the new has come.

2 Corinthians 5:17-18 ESV Therefore, if anyone is in Christ, he is a new creation. The old has passed away; behold, the new has come. All this is from God, who through Christ reconciled us to himself and gave us the ministry of reconciliation;

2 Corinthians 6:14 ESV Do not be unequally yoked with unbelievers. For what partnership has righteousness with lawlessness? Or what fellowship has light with darkness?

2 Peter 1:5-7 ESV For this very reason, make every effort to supplement your faith with virtue, and virtue with knowledge, and knowledge with self-control, and self-control with steadfastness, and steadfastness with godliness, and godliness with brotherly affection, and brotherly affection with love.

2 Samuel 22:31 ESV This God—his way is perfect; the word of the LORD proves true; he is a shield for all those who take refuge in him.

Colossians 2:1-23 ESV For I want you to know how great a struggle I have for you and for those at Laodicea and for all who have not seen me face to face, that their hearts may be encouraged, being knit together in love, to reach all the riches of full assurance of understanding and the knowledge of God's mystery, which is Christ, in whom are hidden all the treasures of wisdom and knowledge. I say this in order that no one may delude you with plausible arguments. For though I am absent in body, yet I am with you in spirit, rejoicing to see your good order and the firmness of your faith in Christ. ...

Colossians 3:14 ESV And above all these put on love, which binds everything together in perfect harmony.

Colossians 3:18-19 ESV Wives, submit to your husbands, as is fitting in the Lord. Husbands, love your wives, and do not be harsh with them.

Colossians 3:19 ESV Husbands, love your wives, and do not be harsh with them.

Colossians 3:2 ESV Set your minds on things that are above, not on things that are on earth.

Do not deprive one another, except perhaps by agreement for a limited time, that you may devote yourselves to prayer; but then come together again, so that Satan may not tempt you because of your lack of self-control.

Ecclesiastes 4:10 ESV For if they fall, one will lift up his fellow. But woe to him who is alone when he falls and has not another to lift him up!

Ecclesiastes 4:10-12 ESV For if they fall, one will lift up his fellow. But woe to him who is alone when he falls and has not another to lift him up! Again, if two lie together, they keep warm, but how can one keep warm alone? And though a man might prevail against one who is alone, two will withstand him—a threefold cord is not quickly broken.

Ecclesiastes 4:12 ESV And though a man might prevail against one who is alone, two will withstand him—a threefold cord is not quickly broken.

Ecclesiastes 4:2 ESV And I thought the dead who are already dead more fortunate than the living who are still alive.

Ecclesiastes 4:9 ESV Two are better than one, because they have a good reward for their toil.

Ecclesiastes 4:9-12 ESV Two are better than one, because they have a good reward for their toil. For if they fall, one will lift up his fellow. But woe to him who is alone when he falls and has not another to lift him up! Again, if two lie together, they keep warm, but how can one keep warm alone? And though a man might prevail against one who is alone, two will withstand him—a threefold cord is not quickly broken.

Ecclesiastes 7:8-9 ESV Better is the end of a thing than its beginning, and the patient in spirit is better than the proud in spirit. Be not quick in your spirit to become angry, for anger lodges in the heart of fools.

Ephesians 4:1-3 ESV I therefore, a prisoner for the Lord, urge you to walk in a manner worthy of the calling to which you have been called, with all humility and gentleness, with patience, bearing with one another in love, eager to maintain the unity of the Spirit in the bond of peace.

Ephesians 4:2 ESV With all humility and gentleness, with patience, bearing with one another in love,

Ephesians 4:2-3 ESV With all humility and gentleness, with patience, bearing with one another in love, eager to maintain the unity of the Spirit in the bond of peace.

Ephesians 4:29 ESV Let no corrupting talk come out of your mouths, but only such as is good for building up, as fits the occasion, that it may give grace to those who hear.

Ephesians 5:2 ESV And walk in love, as Christ loved us and gave himself up for us, a fragrant offering and sacrifice to God.

Ephesians 5:22-23 ESV Wives, submit to your own husbands, as to the Lord. For the husband is the head of the wife even as Christ is the head of the church, his body, and is himself its Savior.

Ephesians 5:22-33 ESV Wives, submit to your own husbands, as to the Lord. For the husband is the head of the wife even as Christ is the head of the church, his body, and is himself its Savior. Now as the church submits to Christ, so also wives should submit in everything to their husbands. Husbands, love your wives, as Christ loved the church and gave himself up for her, that he might sanctify her, having cleansed her by the washing of water with the word, ...

Ephesians 5:25 ESV Husbands, love your wives, as Christ loved the church and gave himself up for her,

Ephesians 5:25-26 ESV Husbands, love your wives, as Christ loved the church and gave himself up for her, that he might sanctify her, having cleansed her by the washing of water with the word,

Ephesians 5:28 ESV In the same way husbands should love their wives as their own bodies. He who loves his wife loves himself.

Ephesians 5:33 ESV However, let each one of you love his wife as himself, and let the wife see that she respects her husband.

Ephesians 6:1-3 ESV Children, obey your parents in the Lord, for this is right. "Honor your father and mother" (this is the first commandment with a promise), "that it may go well with you and that you may live long in the land."

Exodus 20:12 ESV "Honor your father and your mother, that your days may be long in the land that the LORD your God is giving you.

Galatians 5:22-23 ESV But the fruit of the Spirit is love, joy, peace, patience, kindness, goodness, faithfulness, gentleness, self-control; against such things there is no law.

Genesis 2:18 ESV Then the LORD God said, "It is not good that the man should be alone; I will make him a helper fit for him."

Genesis 2:2 ESV And on the seventh day God finished his work that he had done, and he rested on the seventh day from all his work that he had done.

Genesis 2:24 ESV Therefore a man shall leave his father and his mother and hold fast to his wife, and they shall become one flesh.

Hebrews 10:24 ESV And let us consider how to stir up one another to love and good works,

Hebrews 10:24-25 ESV And let us consider how to stir up one another to love and good works, not neglecting to meet together, as is the habit of some, but encouraging one another, and all the more as you see the Day drawing near.

Hebrews 13:4 ESV Let marriage be held in honor among all, and let the marriage bed be undefiled, for God will judge the sexually immoral and adulterous.

James 1:19 ESV Know this, my beloved brothers: let every person be quick to hear, slow to speak, slow to anger;

James 1:19-20 ESV Know this, my beloved brothers: let every person be quick to hear, slow to speak, slow to anger; for the anger of man does not produce the righteousness of God.

John 13:34 ESV A new commandment I give to you, that you love one another: just as I have loved you, you also are to love one another.

John 15:13 ESV Greater love has no one than this, that someone lay down his life for his friends.

John 3:16 ESV "For God so loved the world, that he gave his only Son, that whoever believes in him should not perish but have eternal life.

John 3:16-17 ESV "For God so loved the world, that he gave his only Son, that whoever believes in him should not perish but have eternal life. For God did not send his Son into the world to condemn the world, but in order that the world might be saved through him.

John 3:3 ESV Jesus answered him, "Truly, truly, I say to you, unless one is born again he cannot see the kingdom of God."

Mark 10:9 ESV What therefore God has joined together, let not man separate."

Matthew 19:18-19 ESV He said to him, "Which ones?" And Jesus said, "You shall not murder, You shall not commit adultery, You shall not steal, You shall not bear false witness, Honor your father and mother, and, You shall love your neighbor as yourself."

Matthew 7:12 ESV "So whatever you wish that others would do to you, do also to them, for this is the Law and the Prophets.

Matthew 7:2 ESV For with the judgment you pronounce you will be judged, and with the measure you use it will be measured to you.

Proverbs 10:12 ESV Hatred stirs up strife, but love covers all offenses.

Proverbs 13:20 ESV Whoever walks with the wise becomes wise, but the companion of fools will suffer harm.

Proverbs 17:1-28 ESV Better is a dry morsel with quiet than a house full of feasting with strife. A servant who deals wisely will rule over a son who acts shamefully and will share the inheritance as one of the brothers. The crucible is for silver, and the furnace is for gold, and the LORD tests hearts. An evildoer listens to wicked lips, and a liar gives ear to a mischievous tongue. Whoever mocks the poor insults his Maker; he who is glad at calamity will not go unpunished. ...

Proverbs 17:17 ESV A friend loves at all times, and a brother is born for adversity.

Proverbs 18:22 ESV He who finds a wife finds a good thing and obtains favor from the LORD.

Proverbs 18:24 ESV A man of many companions may come to ruin, but there is a friend who sticks closer than a brother.

Proverbs 19:14 ESV House and wealth are inherited from fathers, but a prudent wife is from the LORD.

Proverbs 22:1 ESV A good name is to be chosen rather than great riches, and favor is better than silver or gold.

Proverbs 22:1-2 ESV A good name is to be chosen rather than great riches, and favor is better than silver or gold. The rich and the poor meet together; the LORD is the Maker of them all.

Proverbs 22:6 ESV Train up a child in the way he should go; even when he is old he will not depart from it.

Proverbs 27:17 ESV Iron sharpens iron, and one man sharpens another.

Proverbs 31:10 ESV An excellent wife who can find? She is far more precious than jewels.

Proverbs 31:10-11 ESV An excellent wife who can find? She is far more precious than jewels. The heart of her husband trusts in her, and he will have no lack of gain.

Proverbs 4:23 ESV Keep your heart with all vigilance, for from it flow the springs of life.

Proverbs 5:18-19 ESV Let your fountain be blessed, and rejoice in the wife of your youth, a lovely deer, a graceful doe. Let her breasts fill you at all times with delight; be intoxicated always in her love.

Romans 12:10 ESV Love one another with brotherly affection. Outdo one another in showing honor.

Romans 12:1-2 ESV I appeal to you therefore, brothers, by the mercies of God, to present your bodies as a living sacrifice, holy and acceptable to God, which is your spiritual worship. Do not be conformed to this world, but be transformed by the renewal of your mind, that by testing you may discern what is the will of God, what is good and acceptable and perfect.

Romans 12:19 ESV Beloved, never avenge yourselves, but leave it to the wrath of God, for it is written, "Vengeance is mine, I will repay, says the Lord."

Romans 12:9 ESV Let love be genuine. Abhor what is evil; hold fast to what is good.

Romans 12:9-10 ESV Let love be genuine. Abhor what is evil; hold fast to what is good. Love one another with brotherly affection. Outdo one another in showing honor.

Song of Solomon 3:4 ESV Scarcely had I passed them when I found him whom my soul loves. I held him, and would not let him go until I had brought him into my mother's house, and into the chamber of her who conceived me.

Song of Solomon 4:1-7:13 ESV Behold, you are beautiful, my love, behold, you are beautiful! Your eyes are doves behind your veil. Your hair is like a flock of goats leaping down the slopes of Gilead. Your teeth are like a flock of shorn ewes that have come up from the washing, all of which bear twins, and not one among them has lost its young. Your lips are like a scarlet thread, and your mouth is lovely. Your cheeks are like halves of a pomegranate behind your veil. Your neck is like the tower of David, built in rows of stone; on it hang a thousand shields, all of them shields of warriors. Your two breasts are like two fawns, twins of a gazelle, that graze among the lilies. ...

Song of Solomon 4:7 ESV You are altogether beautiful, my love; there is no flaw in you.

DEAR MAN is an interpersonal effectiveness skill (Linehan, 2014).

D	Describe the current situation. Stick to the facts. Tell the person exactly what you are reacting to.	Psalm 119:1-176 Blessed are those whose way is blameless, who walk in the law of the Lord! Blessed are those who keep his testimonies, who seek him with their whole heart, who also do no wrong, but walk in his ways! You have commanded your precepts to be kept diligently. Oh that my ways may be steadfast in keeping your statutes! ...
E	Express your feelings and opinions about the situation. Don't assume that the other person knows how you feel.	Proverbs 18:1: "Whoever isolates himself seeks his own desire; he breaks out against all sound judgment." Proverbs 18:2: "A fool takes no pleasure in understanding, but only in expressing his opinion." Proverbs 18:3: "When wickedness comes, contempt comes also, and with dishonor comes disgrace." Proverbs 18:4: "The words of a man's mouth are deep waters; the fountain of wisdom is a bubbling brook." Matthew 22:39: "And a second is like it: You shall love your neighbor as yourself."
A	Assert yourself by asking for what you want or saying "No" clearly. Do not assume that others will figure out what you want. Remember that others cannot read your mind.	Ephesians 4:15 but speaking the truth in love, we are to grow up in all aspects into Him who is the head, even Christ.
R	Reinforce (reward) the person ahead of time (so to speak) by explaining positive effects of getting what you want or need. If necessary, also clarify the negative consequences of not getting what you want or need.	Ecclesiastes 4:9-12 ESV Two are better than one, because they have a good reward for their toil. For if they fall, one will lift up his fellow. But woe to him who is alone when he falls and has not another to lift him up! Again, if two lie together, they keep warm, but how can one keep warm alone? And though a man might prevail

against one who is alone, two will withstand him—a threefold cord is not quickly broken.

Proverbs 27:17 ESV Iron sharpens iron, and one man sharpens another.

Hebrews 10:24-25 ESV And let us consider how to stir up one another to love and good works, not neglecting to meet together, as is the habit of some, but encouraging one another, and all the more as you see the Day drawing near.

| M | Mindful keep your focus on your goals. Maintain your position. Don't be distracted. Don't get off the topic. Speak like a "Broken record." Keep asking for what you want. Or say "No" and express your opinion over and over and over. Just keep replaying the same thing again and again. Ignore attacks. If the other person attacks, threatens, or tries to change the subject, ignore the threats, comments, or attempts to divert you. Do not respond to attacks. Ignore distractions. Just keep making your point. | Philippians 4:6-7: Do not be anxious about anything, but in everything by prayer and supplication with thanksgiving let your requests be made known to God. And the peace of God, which surpasses all understanding, will guard your hearts and your minds in Christ Jesus.

1 Peter 2:9: But you are a chosen race, a royal priesthood, a holy nation, a people for his own possession, that you may proclaim the excellencies of him who called you out of darkness into his marvelous light.

James 1:21: Therefore put away all filthiness and rampant wickedness and receive with meekness the implanted word, which is able to save your souls. |
| A | Appear confident, effective, and competent. Use a confident voice tone and physical manner; make good eye contact. No stammering, | Philippians 4:13. I can do all things through Him who strengthens me.

Hebrews 4:16. Therefore let us draw near with confidence to the throne of grace, so |

whispering, staring at the floor, retreating.

that we may receive mercy and find grace to help in time of need.

Deuteronomy 31:6. Be strong and courageous, do not be afraid or tremble at them, for the Lord your God is the one who goes with you. He will not fail you or forsake you.

2 Corinthians 12:9. Therefore I will boast all the more gladly about my weaknesses, so that Christ's power may rest on me.

2 Timothy 1:7. For God has not given us a spirit of fear, but of power and of love and of a sound mind.

N   Negotiate be willing to give to get. Offer and ask for other solutions to the problem. Reduce your request. Say no, but offer to do something else or to solve the problem another way. Focus on what will work.

Romans 12:18 ESV If possible, so far as it depends on you, live peaceably with all.

1 Corinthians 13:7 ESV Love bears all things, believes all things, hopes all things, endures all things.

1 Corinthians 6:1-20 ESV / 13 helpful votes

When one of you has a grievance against another, does he dare go to law before the unrighteous instead of the saints? Or do you not know that the saints will judge the world? And if the world is to be judged by you, are you incompetent to try trivial cases? Do you not know that we are to judge angels? How much more, then, matters pertaining to this life! So if you have such cases, why do you lay them before those who have no standing in the church? I say this to your shame. Can it be that there is no one among you wise enough to settle a dispute between the brothers, ...

Ephesians 4:32 ESV / 9 helpful votes

Be kind to one another, tenderhearted, forgiving one another, as God in Christ forgave you.

Hebrews 3:6 ESV / 8 helpful votes

But Christ is faithful over God's house as a son. And we are his house, if indeed we hold fast our confidence and our boasting in our hope.

1 Peter 4:8 ESV / 7 helpful votes

Above all, keep loving one another earnestly, since love covers a multitude of sins.

FAST is an interpersonal effectiveness skill to build self-respect (Linehan, 2014).

F	be Fair	Proverbs 16:11 The Lord demands fairness in every business deal.
		Psalm 9:8 He will judge the world with justice and rule the nations with fairness.
		James 3:17 The wisdom that is from above is...without partiality, and without hypocrisy.
		Isaiah 56:1 Keep justice, and do righteousness, for soon my salvation will come, and my righteousness be revealed.
		Leviticus 19:15 Do not pervert justice; do not show partiality to the poor or favoritism to the great, but judge your neighbor fairly.
A	no Apologies	Psalm 51:3, which expresses the need to admit one's transgressions and sin.
		Matthew 5:23-24, which instructs to reconcile with others before offering gifts to God.
		Ephesians 4:32, which commands to be kind, tenderhearted, and forgiving to one another, as God has forgiven us in Christ.
		Luke 11:4, which teaches us to ask God for forgiveness and to forgive those who owe us anything.
S	Stick to values	Hebrews 13:5 - Let your conversation be without covetousness; and be content with such things as ye have: for he hath said, I will never leave thee, nor forsake thee.

Mark 11:25 - And when ye stand praying, forgive, if ye have ought against any: that your Father also which is in heaven may forgive you your trespasses.

Psalm 63:8, ESV My soul clings to you; your right hand upholds me.

Proverb 3:5-6, TPT Trust in the Lord completely, and do not rely on your own opinions. With all your heart rely on him to guide you, and he will lead you in every decision you make.

Matthew 10:31 "Fear not, therefore; you are of more value than many sparrows."

T   be Truthful

Ephesians 4:15 ESV Rather, speaking the truth in love, we are to grow up in every way into him who is the head, into Christ,

Proverbs 12:22 ESV Lying lips are an abomination to the Lord, but those who act faithfully are his delight.

1 John 3:18 ESV Little children, let us not love in word or talk but in deed and in truth.

2 Timothy 2:15 ESV Do your best to present yourself to God as one approved, a worker who has no need to be ashamed, rightly handling the word of truth.

Ephesians 4:25 ESV Therefore, having put away falsehood, let each one of you speak the truth with his neighbor, for we are members one of another.

John 4:24 ESV God is spirit, and those who worship him must worship in spirit and truth."

John 1:14 ESV And the Word became flesh and dwelt among us, and we have seen his glory, glory as of the only Son from the Father, full of grace and truth.

John 8:32 ESV And you will know the truth, and the truth will set you free."

Psalm 25:5 ESV Lead me in your truth and teach me, for you are the God of my salvation; for you I wait all the day long.

John 17:17 ESV Sanctify them in the truth; your word is truth.

James 1:18 ESV Of his own will he brought us forth by the word of truth, that we should be a kind of first fruits of his creatures.

Psalm 86:11 ESV Teach me your way, O Lord, that I may walk in your truth; unite my heart to fear your name.

John 8:31-32 ESV So Jesus said to the Jews who had believed him, "If you abide in my word, you are truly my disciples, and you will know the truth, and the truth will set you free."

GIVE is an interpersonal effectiveness skill (Linehan, 2014).

G	be Gentle	Philippians 4:5: Let your gentleness be evident to all. The Lord is near.

Galatians 5:22-23: But the fruit of the Spirit is love, joy, peace, forbearance, kindness, goodness, faithfulness, gentleness and self-control. Against such things there is no law.

Colossians 3:12: Therefore, as God's chosen people, holy and dearly loved, clothe yourselves with compassion, kindness, humility, gentleness and patience.

Proverbs 15:1: A gentle answer turns away wrath, but a harsh word stirs up anger.

I   act Interested   Philippians 2:3 ESV Do nothing from selfish ambition or conceit, but in humility count others more significant than yourselves.

Philippians 2:4 ESV Let each of you look not only to his own interests, but also to the interests of others.

Romans 12:10 ESV Love one another with brotherly affection. Outdo one another in showing honor.

1 Corinthians 10:24 ESV Let no one seek his own good, but the good of his neighbor.

1 John 4:7-8 ESV Beloved, let us love one another, for love is from God, and whoever loves has been born of God and knows God. Anyone who does not love does not know God, because God is love.

V   Validate   James 1:19 NIV – Everyone should be quick to listen, slow to speak and slow to become angry.

Proverbs 18:2 ESV A fool hath no delight in understanding, but that his heart may discover itself.

Matthew 7:12 ESV So whatever you wish that others would do to you, do also to them, for this is the Law and the Prophets.

<table>
<tr><td>E</td><td>use an Easy manner</td><td>

Matthew 5:16 ESV In the same way, let your light shine before others, so that they may see your good works and give glory to your Father who is in heaven.

Philippians 2:3-4 ESV Do nothing from selfish ambition or conceit, but in humility count others more significant than yourselves. Let each of you look not only to his own interests, but also to the interests of others.

Philippians 2:1-30 ESV So if there is any encouragement in Christ, any comfort from love, any participation in the Spirit, any affection and sympathy, complete my joy by being of the same mind, having the same love, being in full accord and of one mind. Do nothing from selfish ambition or conceit, but in humility count others more significant than yourselves. Let each of you look not only to his own interests, but also to the interests of others. Have this mind among yourselves, which is yours in Christ Jesus, ...

Luke 6:31 ESV And as you wish that others would do to you, do so to them.

2 Corinthians 9:8-11 ESV And God is able to make all grace abound to you, so that having all sufficiency in all things at all times, you may abound in every good work. As it is written, "He has distributed freely, he has given to the poor; his righteousness endures forever." He who supplies seed to the sower and bread for food will supply and multiply your seed for sowing and increase the harvest of your righteousness. You will be enriched in every way to be generous in every way, which through us will produce thanksgiving to God.

</td></tr>
</table>

FOOD

FOOD for the Soul FOOD for the Soul is an Interpersonal Effectiveness validation skill focused upon mindful validation (Houts, 2020).

F	Focus on the inherent worth of the person, whether it is yourself or someone else. Find what is true or valid about the experience, without thinking that you have to agree or approve. Find what makes sense. Validate that.	Luke 6:31 ESV And as you wish that others would do to you, do so to them. 1 Peter 4:8 ESV Above all, keep loving one another earnestly, since love covers a multitude of sins. Colossians 3:12-13 ESV Put on then, as God's chosen ones, holy and beloved, compassionate hearts, kindness, humility, meekness, and patience, bearing with one another and, if one has a complaint against another, forgiving each other; as the Lord has forgiven you, so you also must forgive. Galatians 5:22-23 ESV But the fruit of the Spirit is love, joy, peace, patience, kindness, goodness, faithfulness, gentleness, self-control; against such things there is no law. Romans 12:13 ESV Contribute to the needs of the saints and seek to show hospitality. John 13:34 ESV A new commandment I give to you, that you love one another: just as I have loved you, you also are to love one another.
O	Observe by listening carefully to what is being said with words, expressions, body language. State the unstated by noting what is not being said. Seek verification of inferences. Ask to understand.	Matthew 28:20 ESV Teaching them to observe all that I have commanded you. And behold, I am with you always, to the end of the age." Acts 20:28 ESV Pay careful attention to yourselves and to all the flock, in which the Holy Spirit has made you overseers, to care for the church of God, which he obtained with his own blood.
O	One in the moment. Hold space or time when needed. Do not multitask.	Philippians 2:2 ESV Complete my joy by being of the same mind, having the same love, being in full accord and of one mind.

1 Peter 3:8 ESV Finally, all of you, have unity of mind, sympathy, brotherly love, a tender heart, and a humble mind.

D   Describe the facts of the situation nonjudgmentally; specifically, accurately and proportionally.

John 17:17 ESV Sanctify them in the truth; your word is truth.

Remember the validating yourself is as important as validating others. Validation is the basis of unconditional positive regard and acceptance of the human condition that we all share. Remember that when validating yourself that even if you realize that the thoughts you are having are irrational or based upon a thinking error is important to understand and validate that they exist and they are powerful at the moment. If you are validating others, even if you disagree with their behavior, find something you can empathize with and connect with

FRIENDS

FRIENDS is an interpersonal effectiveness skill focused upon conflict management. The goal is engaging in conflict in ways that support healthy conflict resolution and relationship management (Houts, 2020).

F	Focus only on the issue, situation or problem at hand. To be successful in de-escalation it is important that we meet the person who is having difficulty where they are. Only by accepting where they are can we be of assistance to them in the moment.	Proverbs 16:3 ESV Commit your work to the Lord, and your plans will be established. Proverbs 4:25 ESV Let your eyes look directly forward, and your gaze be straight before you.
R	Respect personal space. Beware that the need for personal space can increase or decrease depending on the individual, age, relationship, vulnerabilities and challenge of the situation.	1 Corinthians 13:4-5 ESV Love is patient and kind; love does not envy or boast; it is not arrogant or rude. It does not insist on its own way; it is not irritable or resentful;
I	Ignore challenges and focus on the needs of the individual in the moment. Choose wisely, what you insist upon. Look for opportunities for flexibility, compromise or negotiation. Remember that sadness and fear often hide behind anger.	John 4:24 ESV God is spirit, and those who worship him must worship in spirit and truth.
E	Empathy transforms interactions. When people are having difficulty, they often just want to be heard, acknowledged and validated. Apologies do not always represent fault but can acknowledge the difficulty or inconvenience another is experiencing.	Colossians 3:13 ESV Bearing with one another and, if one has a complaint against another, forgiving each other; as the Lord has forgiven you, so you also must forgive.
N	Nonthreatening language; how you speak is as important as what you say. Nonjudgment. Behavior affects behavior and if you react defensively to the emotion being displayed others in the interaction are more likely to react in kind. Try to view the situation in a	2 Timothy 2:15 ESV Do your best to present yourself to God as one approved, a worker who has no need to be ashamed, rightly handling the word of truth.

situational context rather than taking it personally. Think of it as a problem to be solved or issue to be dealt with not about finding fault or placing blame.

D   Do not overreact. Calm is always a choice. Rational detachment from intense emotion allows us to better manage conflict. Beware of taking situations personally. Decision making; the most valuable tool you have in a moment of difficulty is time for decision-making. By holding space in the moment, you increase the likelihood that the person having difficulty will self- regulate.

1 Peter 3:15 ESV But in your hearts honor Christ the Lord as holy, always being prepared to make a defense to anyone who asks you for a reason for the hope that is in you; yet do it with gentleness and respect,

S   Set limits. Be clear, simple and developmentally appropriate. Focus on informing. Offer choices. Start with the most positive first. Ensure that you are giving choices and related effects. Be mindful of your tone and intonation. Use positive language and I or situation focused statements whenever possible. Silence is sometimes the most reasonable answer. You do not have to attend every fight to which you are invited.

2 Timothy 1:7 ESV For God gave us a spirit not of fear but of power and love and self-control.

BIG SMART

BIG SMART is an interpersonal effectiveness skill focused upon engaging in new social situations with others who are unknown to us in such a way that allows others to see who we are in order to provide the foundation for building new long-term meaningful relationships. SMART follows up with how to maintain and deepen new and existing relationships (Houts, 2020).

B	Be present. When situations are challenging it is easy to mask or withdraw in an effort to protect yourself, reduce your anxiety or wish away the moment.	Psalm 16:11 ESV You make known to me the path of life; in your presence there is fullness of joy; at your right hand are pleasures forevermore. Philippians 4:6-7 ESV Do not be anxious about anything, but in everything by prayer and supplication with thanksgiving let your requests be made known to God. And the peace of God, which surpasses all understanding, will guard your hearts and your minds in Christ Jesus. Colossians 3:2 ESV Set your minds on things that are above, not on things that are on earth. Romans 12:2 ESV Do not be conformed to this world, but be transformed by the renewal of your mind, that by testing you may discern what is the will of God, what is good and acceptable and perfect. Colossians 3:23 ESV Whatever you do, work

heartily, as for the Lord and not for men,

Proverbs 4:23 ESV Keep your heart with all vigilance, for from it flow the springs of life.

2 Timothy 1:7 ESV For God gave us a spirit not of fear but of power and love and self-control.

I Introduce yourself. All relationships began with an introduction.

2 Timothy 2:15 ESV Do your best to present yourself to God as one approved, a worker who has no need to be ashamed, rightly handling the word of truth.

G Genuine. Be appropriately open, genuine and interested in the moment. Do not mask or fake. Remember that GIVE is skillful. Without the courage to be imperfect, there is no real connection. Give up controlling the situation. Accept your discomfort as discomfort.

Romans 12:9 ESV Let love be genuine. Abhor what is evil; hold fast to what is good.

1 Timothy 1:5 ESV The aim of our charge is love that issues from a pure heart and a good conscience and a sincere faith.

1 Peter 1:22 ESV Having purified your souls by your obedience to the truth for a sincere brotherly love, love one another earnestly from a pure heart,

S   Show up by completely offering your true presence; no multitasking, and share yourself with others. Without sharing who you really are no one can truly know you and you will always feel apart rather than a part.

1 John 4:8 ESV Anyone who does not love does not know God, because God is love.

M   Try to be a matcher, balancing giving and receiving in relationships.

Galatians 5:13 ESV For you were called to freedom, brothers. Only do not use your freedom as an opportunity for the flesh, but through love serve one another.

A   Accept imperfection. There are no genuine relationships without acceptance of imperfection. All human beings are perfectly, imperfect once you accept, allow and practice this fact you increase your ability to engage with others nonjudgmentally with positive unconditional regard.

Ephesians 2:8 ESV For by grace you have been saved through faith. And this is not your own doing; it is the gift of God,

Romans 5:8 ESV But God shows his love for us in that while we were still sinners, Christ died for us.

1 John 4:12 ESV No one has ever seen God; if we love one another, God abides in us and his love is perfected in us.

R   Reevaluate outdated beliefs and grudges. Cultivate your current relationships and mend ones. Be wary of moralistic

Titus 3:5 ESV He saved us, not because of works done by us in righteousness, but according to his own mercy, by the washing of

beliefs, unattainable
expectations and
vicarious dreams
you may be
inflicting upon
others.

T   Talk. Really talk.
Do not take others'
comments or
opinions as a
personal affront to
your own values and
beliefs. Instead of
seeking to win the
moment, argument
or issue seek instead
to increase your
understanding, come
from a place of
gentleness,
curiosity, empathy
and a desire to learn
how the other
person sees and
experiences the
world.

regeneration and renewal of
the Holy Spirit,

Romans 3:23 ESV For all
have sinned and fall short of
the glory of God,

Matthew 7:12 ESV "So
whatever you wish that others
would do to you, do also to
them, for this is the Law and
the Prophets.

Philippians 2:3-4 ESV Do
nothing from selfish ambition
or conceit, but in humility
count others more significant
than yourselves. Let each of
you look not only to his own
interests, but also to the
interests of others.

1 Peter 4:8 ESV Above all,
keep loving one another
earnestly, since love covers a
multitude of sins.

BLUE ROLL

BLUE ROLL is a relationship effectiveness skill focused on managing conflict and increasing effectiveness in dealing with difficult issues and situations (Houts, 2020).

B   Be dialectic, 'both, and,' not right or wrong, black or white.

Romans 3:23 ESV For all have sinned and fall short of the glory of God,

L   Learn what you do not yet know. What you do not yet understand? Others perspectives? Tell me more about why you think that.

James 1:5 ESV If any of you lacks wisdom, let him ask God, who gives generously to all without reproach, and it will be given him.

James 3:17 ESV But the wisdom from above is first pure, then peaceable, gentle, open to reason, full of mercy and good fruits, impartial and sincere.

U   Unplug and take a break when it becomes nonproductive, fatigue or irritability set in. Do not just walk away or hang up. Promise and follow through on an agreement for when to come back together to discuss the issue.

James 3:13 ESV Who is wise and understanding among you? By his good conduct let him show his works in the meekness of wisdom.

E   Equitable. Seek a fair and balanced outcome.

Proverbs 15:33 ESV The fear of the Lord is instruction in wisdom, and humility comes before honor.

Continuing to struggle… then ROLL with it.

R   Reavow your commitment to the relationship and finding a balanced outcome. 'I care about you and I know we can find a way through this so we can both be satisfied.'

Galatians 6:10 ESV So then, as we have opportunity, let us do good to everyone, and especially to those who are of the household of faith.

Romans 13:9 ESV For the commandments, "You shall not commit adultery, You shall not murder, You shall not steal, You shall not covet," and any other commandment, are summed up in this word: "You shall love your neighbor as yourself."

O   Observe. What is being left unsaid? Ask for clarification. If you do not understand, ask.

Galatians 5:22 ESV But the fruit of the Spirit is love, joy, peace, patience, kindness, goodness, faithfulness,

L   Look for commonalities and common ground and speak them to ensure understanding.

1 Peter 3:9 ESV Do not repay evil for evil or reviling for reviling, but on the contrary, bless, for to this you were called, that you may obtain a blessing.

L   Use loving-kindness with all involved; self and others.

Ephesians 4:32 ESV Be kind to one another, tenderhearted, forgiving one another, as God in Christ forgave you.

References

Houts, L. (2020). *CBT - DBT companion for everyday practice: Skills, worksheets &*
Direct Clinical Practice Resources. Amazon.

Linehan, M. M. (2014). *DBT skills training handouts and worksheets* (2nd ed.).

Guilford Publications.

The ESV Study Bible: English Standard Version. Crossway Bibles, 2008.